Transform your Energy – Change your Life

Nichiren Buddhism 3.0

Susanne Matsudo-Kiliani &

Yukio Matsudo

Copyright and disclaimer

ISBN: 978-1533440211

Contents

Foreword

"Everything is energy and that's all there is to it. Match the frequency of the reality you want and you cannot help but get that reality. It can be no other way. This is not philosophy. This is physics." With these words, Albert Einstein introduced a new perspective about reality in relation to energy. For several centuries now spirituality and science have been considered to be two strictly separate areas, as if they had nothing in common with each other. In recent decades, however, new scientific approaches and theories have emerged that incorporate energy and consciousness, such as quantum physics, neuroscience, consciousness research, genetics, heart research, as well as psychotherapy, which confirm many old Buddhist teachings. Thus, we now have the opportunity to build a bridge between science and spirituality. As such, we were interested in investigating whether many concepts and principles of Nichiren Buddhism can be explained when examined in terms of "energy" and "consciousness".

Millions of people worldwide have already had profound and life-changing experiences with the practice of Nichiren Buddhism. The effect of daimoku, i.e. the chanting of the mantra "Nam-myō-hō-ren-ge-kyō" is therefore experienced practically, at different levels and in various fields of our own life. But is it possible to measure the effect of this practice and "make it visible" with modern methods? In this context we were also concerned with the further question of whether the real, tangible changes caused by this practice could be explained as an energetic process. If so, it should be also possible to measure the mind-altering states that occur during the practice of daimoku.

Does to change your own reality actually mean to change your own energy? Are we not connected with each other and with the entire cosmos, so that our essence is of a cosmic-energetic and spiritual nature? All these issues are illuminated in this book primarily under the aspect of "energy" and translated into the terms of the new scientific approaches that are now integrating energy and consciousness.

This book takes a look at some specific concepts of Nichiren Buddhism like "enlightenment" and the "Ceremony in the Air" considering the perspective of quantum physics. This new paradigm enables us to understand that certain spiritual aspects can be explained in terms of energy as the life force that drives us all and that runs everything. This insight opens a new horizon where spirituality and modern science are combined.

Another question we address is what exactly happens energetically in our body and our environment when we chant in front of the Gohonzon. The results of our electrophotonic measurements are shown in this book: There are significant energetic changes in our energy field, our energy centers and our environment when we chant daimoku. But what exactly are our individual energy centers, called chakras, and what areas in our life are affected by them? The evidence based on the results of these energetic measurements are helpful to convince yourself that the chanting of daimoku works.

No matter what it is that you wish to create or manifest into your life – it has to do something with your own energy. This book shows how daimoku may cause a shift in your energetic frequency that changes every aspect of your life. By chanting daimoku you can get yourself in complete energetic alignment with the things you want to attract to your life. By changing your own energy with daimoku, you will soon start seeing evidence of your desires showing up in your reality.

We can positively or negatively affect the energy of our environment. Even the things around us vibrate at a lower frequency when we are in a negative emotional and energetic state. This was revealed by the fascinating research study done by Dr. Masaru Emoto who gave evidence that water is a kind of energy carrier that receives the vibrations of words, characters and even thoughts and feelings, and reflects them in a visible form. In this book we will show you a beautiful water crystal that reflects the energy of daimoku. Since your body is made up of mostly water, it makes a big difference whether it reflects the pattern of negative emotions or whether it is transformed by the energy of daimoku.

In order to build a concrete bridge between Nichiren Buddhism and some modern points of view, we will first go directly back to its Japanese roots. This form of Buddhism is named after Nichiren, a 13th century Japanese monk who lived from 1222-1282. For more than one decade we have been very fortunate to be able to repeatedly visit the historic sites in Japan where Nichiren spent his life. Going back to the roots of Nichiren Buddhism, we could deepen our own personal relationship to Nichiren as well as our understanding of his teachings and practice.

This book was mainly written in the perspective of Susanne Matsudo-Kiliani, whereas Yukio Matsudo acted as co-writer and invaluably contributed his deep and extensive knowledge. We would like to thank David Brookes for his extraordinary help in proofreading and editing the English version of this book which was originally written in German and then translated into English. Our deepest thanks also goes to Rick Kulak for designing a really wonderful cover.

Susanne Matsudo-Kiliani and Yukio Matsudo

Chapter 1

Following the Footsteps of Nichiren

Back to the roots

I had been practicing this form of Buddhism for 18 years in Germany and I knew that it had been launched by a Japanese monk called Nichiren. I had read many of Nichiren's writings. His letters had become more and more familiar to me over the years due to the modern interpretation of this practice by SGI president Daisaku Ikeda. I had a very concrete personal reference to this practice and indeed I'd had a lot of positive, life-changing experiences. But the man I originally owed this to was somehow not actually real and still like a stranger to me: Nichiren himself.

Then suddenly an unexpected external circumstance occurred and I ended up precisely where it had all begun: in Chiba in Japan, the prefecture in which Nichiren was born and where he grew up. In 2008, my husband had been sent by his German company to Tokyo and we stayed in his hometown, Kashiwa, which is located in the northern part of Chiba Prefecture.

We were lucky enough to live in the town where my husband had grown up and where he still had friends and family. Thus we were not completely alone, like many other expatriates. Above all it was for us of the greatest benefit that we could practice Nichiren Buddhism with the members of Soka Gakkai, the largest Nichiren-based movement, on a daily basis. We could attend the group meetings and had many opportunities to chant together. They were so kind as to take us to the bigger regional meetings. Not only did they give us a lot of support in practicing together, but they also showed extraordinary kindness and warmth that made our life in Japan easy and wonderful. At the end I felt that I had more tender-hearted friends there than in Germany.

One of the elder members told me that there still existed the site in Kamakura where Shijo Kingo had lived. Kamakura was the capital of the shogunate where Nichiren had started to propagate his teachings. I suddenly had the feeling that I really wanted to get closer to Nichiren and to use my stay in Japan in order to do so. On weekends or on holidays we often went to Kominato, to Seichōji-Temple, where Nichiren had been educated to become a monk as a small boy and where he was later ordained. There is a very beautiful statue of him and we always felt the impulse to go to him personally. We trusted Nichiren whole-heatedly and our relationship with this great Buddhist master was very deep and special. Despite the fact that he had not been around for more than 750 years, this relationship was still present and noticeable. This was the reason why we started to look for Nichiren´s original spirit.

At a crossroad in Kominato

Trying to be close to Nichiren

It took us very often to Kominato, this small harbor town on the Pacific Ocean where Nichiren was born in 1222 AD and where he had spent his childhood. This place had become like a second home for us. Whenever I see that chain of rocks which forms a

At the shore of Kominato

natural border with the sea, I feel that this sight must have been very familiar to Nichiren. He loved Kominato and often described the smell of the sea and the smell of fresh fish and of seaweed. All of this still remains so characteristic of the small harbor town to this very day, continuing to gently pervade the whole landscape.

Every time we came to Kominato we stayed at the traditional Japanese hot springs hotel opposite Nichiren's birth temple. This *onsen* (hot spring) was particularly dear to me. I could lie on the open roof of the hotel in a hot spring bath and, overlooking the ocean, I could see my beloved chain of rocks of Kominato. Looking at them always con-nects me deeply to Nichiren. Whenever I was seated in this hot spring roof pool taking in this view, a panorama of such significance to me, I felt as if I had always

Hot spring roof bath on the top of the hotel

known this sight. I could emotionally relate to Nichiren's feeling of being homesick and the longing he felt for his hometown whilst he was in exile. I loved this onsen very much. Afterwards I felt deeply relaxed and enjoyably tired.

Nichiren's birth temple with a statue of Zennichimaro

The nice thing about a traditional Japanese style hotel is that there is no need to dress up for evening dinner, as it is brought and beautifully presented to you in your own room where you can eat it comfortably dressed in a *yukata*, a sort of dressing gown which most Westerners might easily mistake for a kimono.

One evening, whilst taking a bath outside the room, our futons were unrolled on the floor. We went to sleep early in the evening in order to get some sleep, for we wanted to get up at 4 o´clock at the latest to take the car up the

mountain to Seichōji temple, daimoku's place of origin; the place where Nichiren recited Nam-myō-hō-ren-ge-kyō for the very first time at the sunrise of April 28th, 1253 AD. Of course, we also wanted to do this at sunrise and every time we went there, we asked the precise time of sunrise for the next morning, in order to make sure we would be there on time.

Very early in the morning the alarm clock went off and we got up and left the hotel. Of course it was still dark outside and on our way to the temple we first drove to the 24-hour convenience store Seven Eleven and bought a can of hot coffee. That helped against the tiredness and the cold. Inwardly, we were very excited and filled with positive anticipation. The blue of the dark night is much stronger there than in Germany, where I was raised. In the distance I could hear the elongated sound of the cawing crows that were beginning to prepare for the break of day.

The ride up the mountain always felt truly magical. Arriving at the temple was even more mysterious. Here I also noticed the tinny sound of crows and I could see the silhouette of the red entrance gate, through which the first rays of sunlight fell as well as the outlines of the main hall of the temple.

The scents of cedar wood and fresh greenery filled the forest. Walking along the forest path we came along a thousand-year-old cedar tree Nichiren must have been familiar with when he lived here.

The grave of Dōzenbō

On the opposite side of this old tree there is the grave of Dōzenbō, Nichiren's mentor at Seichōji temple, for whom Nichiren felt so much compassion in later years. I felt that the whole area, all the trees and every branch, every stone and every path, was soaked with **daimoku**, which has been recited here outdoors, daily, for centuries.

We hurried up the stone steps and the subsequent forest path up to the statue of Nichiren, which is located exactly at the point where for the first time he recited **daimoku** to the Pacific Ocean more than 750 years ago. This place is called "Asahigamori", which means "forest of the morning sun."

Asahigamori: Daimoku's place of origin

A magical place called Asahigamori

After we had reached the end of the steps, Nichiren's figure appeared majestically through the dawn, standing there on the mountain top. This statue radiates an unbelievable strength, certainty, clarity and steadfastness. Every time he stood like this, nothing could knock him down. For us it was always like a direct encounter with this master: this statue stood lofty and clear, stable and safe, the features of his face friendly yet full of decisiveness. His view was directed over a huge forest towards the Pacific Ocean in direction of the rising sun. For us it was a place of safety and a place of coming home. Every time, we felt Nichiren's energy and we communicated directly with him. I talked to him and told him all my problems and sorrows – I got an answer every time. I felt completely accepted and secure so that I could open my heart and keep it full of trust.

In front of us we saw the magical play of the morning sun which was rising slowly over the Pacific Ocean, forming a reddish aura. Deeply moved and focused, we started to recite the second and the sixteenth chapter of the Lotus Sutra and recited **daimoku** until the sun had completely risen. After 20 years of Buddhist study, Nichiren came to the conclusion that the recitation of **daimoku** (**Nam-myō-hō-ren-ge-kyō**) was the core of all Buddhist teachings. That was the point when he publicly proclaimed his revolutionary teaching in the main hall of Seichōji temple on April 28th, 1253 AD. Here everything had begun. I felt as if I too could completely start from scratch again, as if I could design my life in a completely new way. And so it was ….

You just could not kill Nichiren

I realized over time that among all the people who had a significant impact on my life, the man who lived in Japan in the 13th century, known as Nichiren, is the one who caused the most radical change of my mindset and my self-image. I first encountered him in his writings, and then in Japan at all the places where he had lived and where he had overcome difficult and life-threatening situations in an almost superhuman way. Only in Japan itself, in Kamakura, on the island of Izu, in Minobu, on the island of Sado and in Tatsunokuchi, the place where the attempt to behead Nichiren happened, did I powerfully realize that all of this had *actually* happened. He really must have had access to a higher power in order to survive and to overcome all these seemingly insurmountable threats. *You just could not kill him.*

One of the Japanese members told me that one of her friends still had letters of one of his ancestors, who had been present as a soldier during the attempt to behead Nichiren in Tatsunokuchi. In one of his letters he reported about the miraculous incident

Tatsunokuchi

that Nichiren could not be killed, as a radiant heavenly body appeared above the island of Enoshima. At this moment something inside of me changed, and I suddenly realized that up until then I had read all of Nichiren's writings - which he had left for posterity and which have been handed down as his "Gosho" - in a rather metaphorical way, similarly to how I used to read the Bible: more like a beautiful legend about a hero or a saint.

No one could kill Nichiren in Tatsunokuchi!

I was deeply agitated and it became clear to me that Nichiren's experiences were no legends and I realized that the miraculous experiences of Nichiren had *actually* occurred that way. I was burning with curiosity and longing.

It was my husband who took me to this particular site in Kamakura, where Tatsunokuchi had formerly been. We also saw the rock on the island of Izu, Nichiren's place of  exile, where he had been left to die. We discovered this rock by accident. We had driven up to Izu and taken a taxi, which was supposed to take us to the sea near the beach where Nichiren had been exposed on a rock. His persecutors hoped that he would drown when the water rose at high tide. But even there Nichiren was saved by a miracle: the random passing of a fishing boat. We told the taxi driver that we were looking for the rock on which Nichiren had been exposed. He told us that a large statue of Nichiren had been built exactly on that rock. We asked the taxi driver to take us to this statue.

We were very surprised that by chance we ended up once again at the exact spot we had actually been looking for. I was deeply touched because once more I realized how hopeless Nichiren's initial situation had been and to which extent he had transformed this dangerous situation. You just could not kill him. He was also able to turn around situations where anyone else would have given up.

Why was Nichiren persecuted?

What had actually happened? I asked myself this question again and again. Why was Nichiren so vehemently persecuted by the rulers of his time? Well, it was quite simple. He could no longer bear the suffering of the people around him. His time was marked by huge disasters. One earthquake followed another; people were injured and suffering from hunger; and, moreover, the country was threatened by war. The Mongols were at the gates of Japan, trying to conquer the country. This was a serious threat for they had already managed to conquer Northern China and Korea. Would Japan be able to stop them? Nichiren knew that there was an antidote to this misery. He was so strongly convinced of the transformative energy of daimoku that would transform this misery and restore peace across the country.

> He knew that the power of daimoku was
> stronger than any secular law.

For this reason he did something incredible. He called the rulers and influential spiritual leaders of his time to adopt his teachings in order to ensure peace in his country. Therefore, he presented the powerful Shogunate and some influential Buddhist temples with his writing "Rissho Ankoku Ron", the "writing to secure peace in the country by establishing the right dharma". In this case the word "dharma" meant the mantra of "Nam-myō-hō-ren-ge-kyō". That was extremely daring, and Nichiren knew it. He had criticized those in power. He stood alone and had no supporting institution behind him. He was only equipped with his compassion to free the people from hunger, illness, natural disasters and the threat of war. He had the courage to challenge the establishment. By doing so, he wanted to reach a turning point in the policy of the rulers of his time in order to stop the misery and the suffering of the people. He knew exactly what this meant. He would be relentlessly hunted and persecuted from then on, for no ruler of his time would let anyone who dared to criticize him go unpunished. Despite this, Nichiren had such a deep trust in his teachings and was so firmly convinced about the power of daimoku that he did it regardless.

I began to understand the extent and significance of his experiences. I could not explain, though, how he could have mastered all these critical situations under normal conditions. How could he survive all those attacks? How did he survive the two raids on his hut in the outskirts of Kamakura, and the dangerous attack in Komatsubara when he visited his sick mother? How did he manage?

Chapter 2
From the Ego to the Higher Self

Radical change of one´s own self image

I have been reading Nichiren's writings again and again. *"Never seek this Gohonzon outside yourself."* The Gohonzon is a mandala originally inscribed by Nichiren as an object for meditative focus. For years, I had noticed that I was not putting this sentence into practice, nor did I really understand it. Again and again, I tried to use the personal power of my limited ego-consciousness, which constantly felt afraid, to change things on the outside, until I really understood deeply that this sentence also included the demand to radically change one´s own self-image.

How is it that so many people are not capable of really changing and improving their lives, even though they have been working on themselves very hard for years? What if we did not have to "improve" at all, because our self is already complete? What if we did not have to struggle to achieve something, because we already have everything? Did Nichiren not say that we are "fully equipped" and that we can activate and unfold Buddhahood naturally? What exactly did he mean? And what exactly is "Buddhahood"? This was a question I asked myself over and over again. I began to understand that these two statements constituted the missing link that explained what often prevented me and others from experiencing real change.

I understood that my deepest desires did not represent anything external that I could reach out and obtain, but that my desires had something to do with my inner state of consciousness that tried to unfold from within. Was the *Gohonzon* a means to achieve a higher state of consciousness?

Nichiren talks about how "deep down we are already enlightened beings" who have what you might call a "higher self" and who are connected to cosmic consciousness. This is our true consciousness, which is absolutely free from all the burdens of our everyday selves or our "small egos". Daisaku Ikeda also emphasizes the difference between the "small ego" and the "greater self," which we call the "higher self." In this way, we already have an unlimited potential. I began to understand what it's all about when we chant in front of the Gohonzon. It means to unfold this potential quite naturally, because this enlightened unlimited self appears much more strongly and clearly on the outside the more one activates this state of consciousness on the inside. Nichiren had activated this higher enlightened self completely. Here we are facing a real paradigm shift which encourages us to drastically change our self-images.

To change your life does not mean to become
different from who you are
but to activate and unfold your higher self

We are spiritual beings

Nichiren describes our identity with a metaphorical image of the Lotus Sutra. He referred to those who recite daimoku as the "Bodhisattvas of the Earth" who are already enlightened in their deepest inner core. He is saying nothing more than that we are spiritual beings who are here on earth but who come from "an empty space below this earth". This term is metaphorical for enlightenment. We come from an enlightened level, from pure, enlightened consciousness. At this level, which is absolutely different from our daily life, we are free from any classification like being a man or a woman, being a parent or a child, being a boss or a subordinate. Moreover, we are not affected by the wounds from the past and we do not worry about the future. At this level we are just energy and of spiritual nature, that is, pure consciousness.

Everything else, such as our bodies, our performances, our financial situation, our successes, our possessions, even our relatives and our children, are aspects of a world that is constantly changing and eventually dissolving. But according to our true nature we are boundless, infinite beings that come from a source that is itself unchanging and eternal: the enlightened cosmic consciousness. We are purely spiritual beings. Up until that point, I had been thinking that I was a human being having a spiritual experience, but now I realized that my true identity was somehow different.

As a Bodhisattva of the Earth
I come from the realm of enlightenment, that is,
I am a spiritual being having a human experience.

In this case "spiritual" does not mean any particular religious orientation but a fundamental dimension that is hidden behind everyday reality. When we are connected with this level, we feel deeply connected with other people, with nature and with our environment. But what exactly is "enlightenment" and how do I have to practice in order to truly experience it? This was simply a concept I had not grown up with and which I really wanted to experience and understand. I felt this dimension every time I chanted **daimoku** intensively.

Often I had heard about the distinction between our "bigger, higher self" and our "small ego", but somehow this remained theoretical and abstract to me, which I could believe in or not. I read countless books and explanations about these concepts, but then I came across a book written by Anita Moorjani who had experienced an almost incredible near-death experience. Reading her descriptions helped me to classify my own experiences much better. Suddenly I understood what the "higher self" really was. I realized that there were basically two versions of myself: my human self and my essential energetic higher self. Anita's experience helped me understand that it was my life´s purpose to overcome this separation.

A spiritual near-death experience

Anita was dying of cancer, and when her organs failed she was told that she still had less than 36 hours to live. Then she fell into a coma and her body was already in the process of dying. In the course of her near-death experience she realized that *"everything that happens in our lives depends on the energy that surrounds us and that was created by us. Nothing is fixed – we are the creators of our environments and our conditions in*  *life which depend on how we use this energy. Our physical body gets ill because we live on a certain level of energy"*.

Anita experienced a state of consciousness that she regarded as her true self – a state of unconditional love and acceptance. During this process she realized that if she went back to life

Susanne meeting Anita Moorjani in Basel, Switzerland, in September 2016

then it would be with a completely healthy energy, because now she *"had realized who she truly was and understood the wonderful dimension of her true self*". Her physical body would soon catch up. Anita got the chance to go back to her body, which had been devastated by cancer. And yet, four days after her near-death experience, she did not show any more signs of cancer. The doctors declared her body to be completely cancer-free only three weeks afterwards. The doctors were completely stunned, because they did not think that such a thing was possible and they had no medical explanation for it. Even if her cancer was cured, it could not just disappear within four days. According to common medical knowledge this would take at least six months. But Anita knew that she was cured and up to now it cannot be explained in medical terms how her cancer could have disappeared in only four days.

She realized that her cancer had disappeared through an altered *state of being*, which means an altered *state of consciousness*. This leads to a new energy that causes changes in all areas of life, not only curing diseases. At the specific level of consciousness, she had during her experience Anita realized the following:

> "*We can change our physical reality*
> *when we change our energy.*"

This moving experience is portrayed by Anita in her book "Dying To Be Me" (2012). What moved me the most, however, was that what she described confirmed that, independently from our everyday self, we do actually have a higher self that is unlimited and connected with everything. All aspects Anita had described made sense to me. Those were ideas which corresponded to the ideas I had been familiar with in Nichiren Buddhism. She described them in a way, however, that helped me understand the deeper meaning of what Nichiren had always been trying to say in a more metaphoric manner.

Our true self

Anita´s experience made her question her former self-image

completely, because she experienced that not only our body
and our everyday-self constitute
our true self, but that there is
another dimension where we do
have a higher self, which she
herself described as *"limitless"*. At
this level she felt *"an astonishing
beauty and freedom of the other
world"*. Nichiren called this
deepest level of life *"the palace of
the ninth consciousness of*

unchanging truth," which is pure consciousness free of any karmic
influence and which governs all life functions.

At this dimension we are one with the whole universe
and may create miracles in our everyday lives.

Anita had become aware that she was more than just her body,
for she had left her body. She knew that there was another part
of her, which she experienced as a *"limitless great being"* that, in
this state, merged with pure consciousness. She understood that
her body was just a mere reflection of her inner state and that
healing would occur by connecting to her true self. This true self
had nothing to do with her everyday consciousness, which had
been conditioned by her experiences from the past. It was *pure
consciousness*. *"My great limitless self had decided to go on living
and to express itself through this body, thus nothing in this world
could interfere with this decision"*.

Anita describes the true self as independent of our body, our
culture, our gender, our race and of religious dogmas. I thought of

Nichiren, who knew that at this level of the higher self there is no more duality and we are no longer limited by social or cultural conditioning. Didn´t he say: *"There should be no discrimination among those who propagate the five characters of Myō-hō-ren-ge-kyō in the Latter Day of the Law, be they men or women"* (»The True Aspect of All Phenomena« of 1273).

Once again I was deeply impressed that already in the 13th Century Nichiren had consistently fought for equality between men and women, while many other religious leaders have failed to do so until today.

But what exactly was this higher self? According to Anita, her true self was *"far more powerful"* and *"in no way broken or damaged."* I was intrigued. In these sentences I recognized the double structure of human life described by Nichiren, which stated that on one side we are a normal everyday man and woman with nine life states; and, at the same time, a spiritual, enlightened being and therefore we have the ability to transform everything negative into something positive. A "Bodhisattva of the Earth", as appears in the "Ceremony in the Air", is characterized precisely by this double structure.

You are a normal everyday man or woman
whose true identity is a spiritual, enlightened being.

Our higher self fuses with universal energy

Anita Moorjani´s description, *"in no way broken or damaged,"* reminded me of the "Lotus essence" of the Bodhisattvas of the Earth described by Nichiren, whose essence is comparable to a symbolically pure lotus flower since this essence is not soiled by worldly affairs and therefore remains free of impurities.

I had never read a description of this enlightened self before. But in Anita's words I realized the resonance with Nichiren's words, and I was infinitely grateful that I did not need a near-death experience to get in touch with my higher self. Anita Moorjani had to almost lose her life in order to become aware of her higher self and in order to experience this condition. But Nichiren left us his mandala to enter this higher state of being which is already inscribed in the mandala. In the center of the mandala is the energetic signature that contains this enlightened state. By activating Nam-myō-hō-ren-ge-kyō the enlightened struc-ture of the entire cosmos and every single human being is brought to light. Through chanting, I really get a completely new identity. In this sense:

We experience an initiation during each daimoku recitation
before the Gohonzon, in which the old ego of everyday
life dies and the new cosmic self is activated and unfolds.

Anita realized that her limitless self hosted all the resources she needed to navigate through life, because in this state she was "*one with the universal energy*". This description corresponds exactly to the concept of "being perfectly equipped", which is one of the characteristics of "Myō" (the mystical). Suddenly many concepts, which I had heard so often before, came to life. Anita Moorjani considers the oneness with this universal energy, which is charac-terized by absolute clarity, the cause of her healing, which was accomplished at that level and which later manifested in her body.

She described one aspect of this universal life energy to be the amazing, overwhelming and indescribable clarity one feels in this state of life and with which one perceives one's life and the relationships therein. This also reminded me of the incredibly clear feeling that arises during intensive **daimoku**. Anita describes this state as the *"stunning beauty and freedom"* of the other world. Universal energy in this case means "life force energy", which is the source of all life and which flows through every living being. By connecting to this universal life energy we are fully equipped with all potentialities. This is exactly what Nichiren described in the principle of ichinen-sanzen. Once we are connected to the level of our enlightened pure consciousness and to universal life energy, then we can make changes on the physical plane. But mostly we are not on this level of consciousness and often we are blocked by limiting ideas about ourselves and our lives. But if we do not recognize our own essence, then we deny our own magnificence. Thus, when we refer to the level of your being we call higher self, we are referring to the source and essence of all life. Your higher self is your eternal, infinite consciousness that fuses with universal life energy, free from all attachments; it is constant and unchanging, birthless and deathless.

This higher self can be only known through direct experience. It cannot be experienced through the rational mind.

When you are connected to your higher self, you can express the energy and the light of this unlimited consciousness through your words, thoughts, actions and all that you are and do at the personal level. You are being your higher self every time you align with this unlimited consciousness and carry out its goals.

Exercise 1

If someone told you that you are magnificent, powerful, amazing and beautiful beyond measure, how would you feel?

- -

Do you receive it with an open heart? Or do you resist by thinking that you're not THAT beautiful and magnificent?

Don't act against your true self!

Our problems arise when we are in a restricted state of consciousness, which then becomes the basis of our thinking and acting. Anita Moorjani, too, became aware during her near-death experience that she had become ill because she had "denied" herself. She realized that her constant fear had made her sick in the end. *"During my near-death experience I had the feeling that condemnation, hatred, envy, jealousy and fear come from people who do not realize their true greatness. Our lack of awareness about our own perfection makes us constantly feel small and insignificant and that contradicts the natural flow of life-force energy – this is what we really are. We oppose ourselves."*

She understood that the ignorance of her own unlimited great self and her negative emotions had sickened her at the end. *"I did not express my true self because my fears and concerns prevented me from doing so. I understood that the cancer was not a punishment or anything like that. It was just my energy which manifested itself as cancer, because my fears did not allow me to express this great power which I was supposed to be."*

My experiences with the Gohonzon and Anita's description of her near-death experience made it very real to me that we do have a higher self and that the state of "Buddhahood" was an energetic state to which we align ourselves by practicing daimoku in front of the Gohonzon. This state is already inscribed in the Gohonzon. I understood: as soon as I align my own energetic level with the energetic signature of the Gohonzon or my higher self, the more this state will appear in my life, and the more this energy flows through me. This was the basis of the first major paradigm shift Nichiren asked me to do: to realize that I had a magnificent, limitless higher self in me which corresponded to a limitless state of freedom, joy, happiness, connectedness and love. It depended on me to which extent I let this state appear in my life. I just had to align to this state and express this higher consciousness through me. But one thing was sure: I did not have to look on the outside for answers any more, but I had to repeatedly make it clear to myself that I actually have this dimension or force which I can activate via practicing **daimoku.**

> Everything is in me. Whatever is missing is
> what I am not giving or activating or unfolding.

Is your ego or your higher self speaking?

Sometimes we are so caught up in our everyday restricted aware-ness that we do not have access to the incredible opportunities that lie beyond it. We are limited to our specific local and temporal existence. This restricted everyday consciousness is often referred to as "local consciousness" or "local self" because we perceive everything in our life from our personal and individual perspective limited in the specific dimension of space and time. It contains our ego in the form of our self-defined "I", which goes through life dependent on our conditioned habits. This local awareness inher-ently separates us from the rest of the world. But how do you always know what mode you are operating in?

So how can you tell if you are in the ego mode? Sometimes you can even be happy in ego mode. You can feel very important, secure and envied. You might even feel loved and respected. But there is one way you know for sure if you are in ego-mode: If you are struggling. The satisfaction we get out of ego mode never comes easily. You have to work very hard for satisfaction or approval. You are stressed most of the time to get everything working the way that you want it to. You want to be successful. You want to be the perfect partner. You want to be the perfect mother. You want to be perfect in your job. We constantly push ourselves beyond our limits. You have to constantly push yourself.

Your human, local self lives through all the experiences that make you feel a victim. Very often, that feeling is true: Your human self has been abandoned, betrayed, lied to, neglected, hurt, wrongly accused and judged. On this level, you sometimes may feel the separation from universal life energy as very painful.

In ego mode we cannot be loving with ourselves unless we feel that we have earned it. We give up our needs and desires in order to serve everybody else. You put other people first. We believe that love must be earned by proving how good and nice we are. We are therefore always busy trying to earn love and approval on the outside. We think that we have to lose weight, that we have to earn more money or be a better Buddhist, in order to be loved or approved or even admired. We come from a place of scarcity. Deep down we think we are not worthy or good enough or that our situation is hopeless.

In ego mode we are trying to fix and control things.

But we are not able to create a new situation, because we are in a restricted awareness, cut off from all other possibilities. In everyday life we are often in our "local consciousness". We believe that *we* are the ones who control things. Similarly, we believe that it depends solely on ourselves and our own strength if we want to achieve something. This often causes anxiety and stress, of course.

What if I cannot do it? What if everything goes wrong? What if I am not good enough? These are the questions our "local self" is constantly asking. Even if we practice we can often remain trapped in our local consciousness. That is the case when we do not really connect to our "non-local" consciousness or higher self. Because only through this connection does our local consciousness experience itself as integrated into non-local consciousness.

When you are connected to your higher self, then you know that everything is possible at any moment, because you have access to all possibilities. When you are operating in the mode of your everyday ego-self you often think that to change your situation, relating to your relationship or your finances for example, "is not possible". Furthermore, you seem afraid and convinced that you have "to do a lot" or that you have to change in order to be loved. You think that you first have to lose that weight, overcome your insecurity, earn more money, and *then* you can be loved. You feel undeserving and unworthy. Connected to the energy of your higher self, however, you feel that you are always loved and supported. In ego-mode, you might feel as if the whole world is acting against you in certain ways. You resist change, because you assume that change means that things will get worse. You often have regrets about the past or anxieties about the future. Connected to your higher self, you know with confidence that if things are changing, it signifies that universal life energy is making space for things to get better.

This is exactly what our journey in returning home to connect with the energy of our higher self is: aligning those parts of us to the frequency of the higher self that are experiencing fear, anger and grief. As we bring in our higher self, we help the essential energy that we truly are to raise our human experience, ours and everybody else's around us.

For it is the universal, non-local self
which coordinates all events in your life.

But what are the conditions to ensure that this connection is made? Which conditions must be fulfilled in order to do so? Because just as the cherry stone already contains the cherry tree, so our self contains everything it needs in order to fulfil its higher purpose – but only as *potential*. The cherry stone requires certain factors and conditions in order to grow and to develop to a cherry tree. The truth is: not every cherry stone becomes a cherry tree. So what are the conditions required?

The inner conditions for activating your higher self

Nichiren describes the emer-
gence of the enlightened self
evoked by mantra meditation
in front of the Gohonzon as a
natural process that occurs in
a simple way, as is the case
with a baby who is nourished
by being breast-fed by its

mother. The baby has full confidence in the mother and does not reflect on the process or the ingredients of the milk. Whenever Nichiren stresses the importance of "believing" in the Gohonzon, he means exactly this principle of naturally activating and unfolding the potentiality of Buddhahood or our true nature. He mentions also that this development process is as natural as the growth of a bird's egg. At the beginning it only consists of liquid and then, being warmed by its mother, it quite naturally develops into a fully equipped bird with a beak and eyes, which is even soon able to fly. He compares us human beings to a *"miserable egg of delusion"*, but once *"warmed up by the reciting mother of Nam- myō-hō-ren-ge-kyō"* we may develop the qualities of a Buddha. Just like the liquid in an egg requires the right conditions, like a certain temperature or warmth in order to grow into a bird, the recitation of the daimoku creates the right *inner* conditions through which the higher self can unfold. Therefore, it doesn't matter which external conditions you are currently exposed to. If you create the right mental, emotional and spiritual conditions, your desired results will manifest in a natural way. What exactly are these right inner conditions?

In order to connect to this higher self, we need to be absolutely trusting and dedicated to the Gohonzon. A baby does not ask itself constantly whether its mother's milk works or not. Only when we open ourselves to the Gohonzon, full of gratitude and trust, will we experience a new dimension of love, forgiveness, and endless possibilities. Only then does our local everyday consciousness recognize the fundamental reality behind everyday phenomena and merges with the higher self. When we give up trying to figure out how or when our desires and our visions will be fulfilled, we leave those details to the higher self that knows so much more than we do. It will answer your prayers to the Gohonzon in a way that will surprise you, to show you that the answer came from a higher consciousness, and that it was not your ego that controlled the outer events in your life.

Our higher self can change external circumstances

Normally we think that the effects we experience depend on circumstances that are beyond our control. However, if we attune ourselves to the perfect pattern of our higher self, which is trying to unfold from within, then outer conditions start moving in the required direction. When I connect to this higher self, people and circumstances will occur in my life that bring me exactly what I desperately needed at that moment – something I could have never arranged solely by using my own power. Your higher self within you is distinct from your "local consciousness", your human existence which was born and has already had certain experiences and which eventually will turn to dust. Your higher self is looking to unfold even further, beyond this. With this understanding of your higher self you are no longer at the mercy of external conditions or your experiences in the past.

You are not a limited physical existence. You are a limitless being. This knowledge will help you to understand a completely new way of understanding your personal reality. You can stop fighting to improve, to manifest or to attract something. If you simply activate this mystical pattern in the depths of your life with **daimoku**, then this higher self unfolds in your life in a powerful, dynamic and life-changing way.

Confrontation with my lousy karmas

This has repeatedly been my experience over the years, in my practice of **daimoku** in front of the Gohonzon. I concretely experienced what it means to get "benefits", as they say. Years ago, I was intensively working on my PhD and desperately needed support because my supervisor had changed to another university and was always very difficult to reach.

At this time, I was very exhausted from the constant struggle for support or even just an appointment to meet my supervisor. Somehow he had come to embody the old situation in my life when, during my first degree, I had often simply longed for more support. I'd had to manage a lot of difficult situations at the same time, since both my parents became seriously ill during my studies and their illness devoured a lot of time, energy and even the entire family fortune.

That's why for years I financed my studies myself under difficult conditions and scratched a living with all sorts of jobs. I was tutoring, I sold furniture to the stationed American soldiers in

Germany, and later during my studies I began to work as a translator. But the entire period of my studies was overshadowed by the illness of my parents. My father had developed Alzheimer's disease in his mid-fifties, and my mother had breast cancer shortly afterwards. Both died within two years of each other, before I had finished my studies. Apart from all these psychological and emotional challenges, I fought my way through the exams and my studies, because I wanted to finish by any means.

What really got to me in this period was the nasty and malicious nature of my brother. If there is something like "lousy karma" in my life, then it was the karma to grow up with a brother who fought my very existence. He had always been morbidly jealous of me, just simply because I had been born to this world. But when my father became ill, he started to fully live out his mean nature.

He not only behaved extremely unkindly to my parents, but he also tried to make life hard for me and to interfere with my studies. He often refused to let me into my parents' apartment when my mother was not in and I simply wanted to visit my sick father. He terrorized my already weakened mother and put her under pressure, because he did not want me to come home any more. It cost my poor mother a lot of strength to stand up to him. He came by at night and was loud and aggressive. Then I just left the apartment so my mother would not be burdened by a dispute even further.

At that time, I was so exhausted that my body reacted violently to it. From one day to the other I developed massive hypothyroidism, which I have had to treat with medication ever since. The two sisters of my mother, who were fortunately there to assist me during my mother's illness, were horrified by my brother's behavior. No one really understood his pathological behavior or why he had to make life more difficult for all of us, especially at this time. But he would have liked to take away even the air that I breathed if he could have. He often shouted out loud that I should "have an accident and die".

The whole situation really got me down. Nevertheless, I had the iron will to study, but I often longed for support in the way my fellow students got support from their parents or family. I used every free minute to earn money. The rest of the time I had to deal with my parent´s situation or to defend myself against my brother´s attacks.

Mystical coincidence of synchronicity

Now all of this was long time ago and I had managed to successfully finish my studies. Due to many years of practice of **daimoku** I also felt no grudge or any sense of powerlessness towards my brother, because I had also managed to set him clear boundaries later on. He had no more influence on my life. I even felt a bit sorry for him, because I deeply realized the negative effects he had on his own life and how insecure he actually was deep down.

Together with my husband I had built up my strength and then challenged myself a few years later to take up a PhD course. But now new difficulties arose, in the form of my supervisor who was not very supportive and who always made it clear that he placed great demands on me since I was doing a doctorate at a very prestigious university. I chanted intensively for the ability to successfully and quickly finish my PhD. That was the time when I happened to make contact with a professor in the United States who was really familiar with my topic. He also happened to be the Vice-Dean of the University and of course had great influence. I had written to him and surprisingly obtained a very quick answer from him.

And here I experienced the incredible interplay of "mystical coincidence of synchronicity", as we call this phenomenon, which occur when we are connected to our higher self. Exactly at this time my husband was invited to give a lecture at an American university and we were simultaneously invited privately by an American friend to stay in Chicago with him and his wife. So there were several reasons and occasions to fly to the US.

When staying at the American university where my husband was giving a lecture, I was delighted with the supportive and positive nature of the Americans in the academic field. I realized that I enjoyed it on the international stage and suddenly felt intensely that I was profoundly worth it and that I deserved to live up to my own potential. I deserved to be treated with respect and good will. I really managed well there and I started to appreciate my own abilities.

I had previously written to the above mentioned American professor in Ohio and had asked him if it was possible to meet him during my planned stay in the US. He responded very quickly that he was ready to meet me. When I arrived in the US, I took the opportunity and made an appointment with him. I was amazed: I immediately got an appointment. This was something I did not necessarily expect after my experiences with several professors in Germany. In Germany I often had to almost beg to get an appointment with my supervisor. Not so in the US.

Furthermore, this American professor offered to send me a chauffeur who would pick me up at the airport in Ohio and who would take me directly to his university. I was completely flabbergasted. I had never experienced anything like that before. A professor who sent a driver to pick me up? That's exactly how it was. The chauffeur picked me up and I got more support and materials for my dissertation from this nice professor than I could have ever imagined. Not only was he a real expert in my topic, but he also provided me with fantastic reports, documents and contacts. They all fit exactly on the subject and were the same crucial aspects I really needed in order to finish my PhD thesis. Finally, the chauffeur took me back to the airport. I thought I had dreamt it all, but this experience shows exactly what I mentioned earlier. It was better than I could have ever imagined before.

I was carried by something far greater than
my personal capacity to make circumstances happen or
to achieve things.

Chapter 3
Surrendering to something great

Be honest to yourself!

As already explained using the example of a bird egg, Nichiren describes the act of activating and unfolding one´s higher self as a kind of law: *Buddhahood appears and unfolds in a natural way.* But it is not always the case that your local and non-local consciousness cooperate. Only if the decisions, thoughts and feelings of the local self are consistent with the non-local self, which is always focused on development and expansion, does a positive change occur in one´s life. If the local self or the everyday ego acts in a way that it contradicts the non-local, higher self, then we feel that very clearly as a negative consequence. Then the non-local consciousness lets us know that our decision was not beneficial to our development.

Especially at the beginning of my practice, I always felt it very strongly when I helped certain people out of a false sense of compassion which was not conducive to their development, and I only felt exploited in the end without any energy left. Then I knew very clearly that this action had not been very conducive for my own development, for I did not feel any energy loss when I helped people who knew how to appreciate me. Therefore I became increasingly honest with myself and denied myself less the longer I practiced.

Much of what we learn throughout our lives takes us paradoxically away from our own self. The constant attempt to improve takes us away from our original perfection and leaves us a feeling as if we are never good enough. This may lead to the situation where we feel even more lacking in our lives.

Exercise 2

Have you noticed that since you started chanting you have become more sensitive towards people and situations?

- -

Do you realize when you take action that you know deep down is not good for you? Describe the specific situation when that has happened to you.

- -

Raise your Energy!

Throughout my Nichiren Buddhist practice I frequently observed that some practitioners tried to use their own power and wisdom to change themselves and to create a new situation on the outside. Sometimes, however, their problems remained the same or got even worse. Then they got a new partner, but the relationship often led back to the old familiar conflicts. Then they got a new job but ended up with the same unbearable boss.

Thus it had to do something with your own specific energy in accordance with your karmic pattern: could it be that one's own energy level influenced the result? If you don't change your own energy, then your own higher self cannot unfold. Then, sooner or later, we act at the level of our everyday ego-consciousness and we are caught up in our karmic pattern. We are solely on a level of "doing" but, due to our old energy level, we keep attracting the same situation as often as we change it. Only when we act at the level of our higher self, real changes happen.

> Being carried by daimoku,
> circumstances will change in synchronicity.

Do not seek this Gohonzon outside yourself

Most of us did not learn at home or at school that we are multi-dimensional beings who, at their deepest level, consist of pure enlightened consciousness. Thus, over the years we have internalized the view that our "I", our everyday ego, is the only center in the world around which everything else rotates. That's the perspective from which we look at the external world, at all events, things and people in our life and from which we seek solutions once we are confronted with difficult situations. Then we seek, as Nichiren put it, *"the Gohonzon outside ourselves"*. Then we seek enlightenment, the source of all solutions and possibilities, in the outer world and not within.

I realized that this sentence means that we think someone or something outside of ourselves could raise our energy and our life state or change the situation we're in and make us happy. This can be our partner, our job, our hobby, the things we own, how we look like or our body. Then it becomes very important how we look, what we own, how much we earn or the role we play in everyday life. For often we deeply believe that we are the happier the more money we have and the more things we own.

At the level of everyday consciousness other people's opinions seem to play a very important role to us. We yearn for recognition and approval and fear rejection because it lets us doubt our own self-image. At this level we have a very limited awareness, which inevitably makes us suffer in the end. Eventually we realize that we fail when we make somebody or something outside our enlightened consciousness the sole source of our happiness.

Exercise 3

Who or what have you been making your source of happiness until now?

- -

- -

- -

You will control everything by your own power?

Our self-image that leads to an outward orientation is, however, very much influenced by what we've learned and experienced in our lives and how other people behaved towards us. Once we have a closer look at this ego, which is based on our self-image, we realize how much fear it feels and how much it is trying to control and dominate things around it: "I have a lot of power and everything is under control and everybody else needs to do what I tell them." Such a scenario gives the ego pure joy at first. But deep down it already feels the nagging fear that the situation could change and that others could do the same. At this level of external object-relatedness we solely identify with external objects, people and situations, and we want them to make us happy.

When you struggle for happiness by solely trying
to change your outer circumstances,
you will remain dependent on them.
That's when they start to control your life.

I experienced this principle very vividly when we were trying to sell our apartment a few years ago. At that time a situation with very hostile neighbors had become almost intolerable. Therefore, we wanted to sell the apartment and build a new house somewhere else. I did everything in my power to realize this: I constantly put ads in local newspapers and I constantly cleaned the apartment, because two or three prospects came to have a look at the apartment almost every weekend. Everybody liked the apartment very well, but no one bought it. This went on for more than six months and I was really at my wits' end. I was obsessed with the idea that I had to *do* many things and really work hard in order to achieve my goal.

Only when all my attempts had failed and when I could not think of anything else to do, did I completely surrender to the Gohonzon. That´s when I only chanted deeply to find a buyer for the apartment. I really had tried everything else and was almost desperate emotionally. I just didn't have any more energy to find a solution and completely handed this matter over to the Gohonzon when I was chanting. With clarity I was holding the image that somebody had already bought the apartment. I completely released the emotion of fear and all the pressure I had put on myself. Suddenly I felt an immense sense of joy and freedom. I just gave up all the solutions I could think of with my limited mind about how this problem should be taken care of. I just trusted in the outcome and allowed this all-knowing higher intelligence to take over and provide the best solution for me.

In the same week, a prospective buyer who had looked at the apartment more than half a year ago called again and said he wanted to buy the apartment, as our apartment turned out to be the best apartment he had seen for the price. I understood – I had given up my ego´s control. I had released my own strategy and left it completely up to the invisible power of my higher, enlightened self in the form of the Gohonzon to find a solution – and it had answered. Now I really understood. This invisible power is real and can organize the events in my life in a way that is perfect for me. This is exactly as Daisaku Ikeda puts it in one of his selected lectures on the Gosho, "The Strategy of the Lotus Sutra": *"Employ the strategy of the Lotus Sutra before any other"* (»Letter to Shijō Kingo« of 1279).

In this lecture he writes that the strategy of the Lotus Sutra refers to completely trusting the Gohonzon and that this trust has the power to break through our negative karma.

When we use the "strategy of the Lotus Sutra,"
we are not trying to control our reality any more.
Instead we are surrendering to something greater.

Letting go!

It meant to allow the leadership of the higher self and to let universal life energy flow through you instead of chasing things on the level of everyday consciousness. When we chase after the things we want, we experience ourselves as separate. The solution lies in the act of allowing based on the confidence in the Gohonzon and not on hectic activities that are more influenced by the fear of not being able to obtain or achieve something. Only through allowing will our own actions lead to the desired results.

We should not only rely on our own power,
nor on external power alone.

But we only get to the level of the higher self when we are open to a radically new notion of ourselves. Nichiren asks you to go beyond your idea of yourself as an ordinary human being, *beginning with a new self-identity*. The question is whether you trust your own fearful ego or your own limitless self. Anita Moorjani describes this process of surrendering as follows: *"The first step of*

surrendering is trust, the second that I always stay true to my true ,
*nature. This way I just attract what is really mine and everything
happens at a speed that suits me. Of course I can constantly think
about the things I worry about or which I still need in my opinion
or what I supposedly lack, but then my life will not move to the
experiences that I would like to make. It will simply remain as it is
now, because I focus my attention on my fears and on the things
that leave me dismayed or unfilled, instead of expanding my
awareness by trusting and allowing new experiences. It is up to me
whether the picture manifests slower or faster, depending on how
fast I am able to give up my worries and relax to open up for the
process."*

The pattern of your magnificent self

What I really understood in the course of my practice with **daimoku**
was that it is not just about increasing your own energy state, but
above all to increase one´s consciousness about *who you really
are.*

All day long we all have thoughts and feelings about ourselves.
Constantly we tell ourselves stories about who we are, what we
are and what we are capable or not capable of doing. We think
about the things we have done or would like to do. How often
have we decided to do something in the past and have not gone
through with it?

But what if there was a lot more in yourself than you could ever ,
imagine? And what if you were more capable than you ever
thought possible? Nichiren calls us "a Bodhisattva of the Earth"
that comes from "the empty space of enlightenment". This pattern of the higher self, which is within us, wants to express and
expand itself through us.

When I expand my own consciousness by practicing **daimoku**
before the Gohonzon, then I leave my everyday consciousness and

deepen my connectivity with the higher self in this meditative process. How strong this connectivity is, depends on the depths of my meditative practice. When we approach this higher self within us, when we adjust to it and act on its behalf, then we are bigger than anything we have known or experienced so far.

This exactly is the reason why Nichiren inscribed the Gohonzon; his mandala allows us to enter that realm where you determine your life much more than you can imagine. For Nichiren tells us very clearly: There is a level of consciousness where we can fulfill any wish.

Practicing to this mandala enables us to reach this wonderful state of being which goes beyond anything we consider "normal." This is where our perception is limitless and free. This consciousness is extraordinary, because it is part of universal consciousness, which is infinite. This part has no limitations and restrictions, but only wants to expand in freedom. As long as we try to solve our problems by the same limited consciousness that created them, we will not get any further. However, when we connect to our limitless higher self, then we experience an inner peace and fulfillment that is no longer dependent on external circumstances but supported by the force of the entire universe.

Exercise 4

Do you ever feel frustrated when you chant a lot and still don´t seem to get the results you were expecting?

- -

What could be the reason for this?

- -

What is "Ichinen"?

Another aspect I wanted to understand was a term that in Nichiren Buddhism is called "ichinen." For a long time, I thought that "ichinen" just meant my determination to strengthen my own will. I often chanted in a very determined and resolute way, sometimes until I was almost hoarse, in order to achieve my goals. I often tried to reinforce my ichinen. But I felt that I still had more to learn about what this expression means and where it came from, because it was often conveyed to me that I activate and reinforce my own inner psychological power by the practice of reciting daimoku. Therefore, I thought I would form my life with my own strength and power.

Ichinen is most often used as a short form of "ichinen- sanzen" which actually describes also the enlightened state of your life inscribed in the Gohonzon. I tried to understand the literal meaning. The word "ichi" means "one". The Chinese character for "nen" consists of two characters. The top one means "now" or "presence" and the bottom one means "heart".

Thus, "ichi nen" is simply "complete presence of heart". It comes when you stop living in your head and stop thinking about the things that you still have to do. That is when you experience complete connection to this present moment in a meditative state, this moment alone and not any other. You are fully tuned into the here and now. You are not experiencing with your everyday consciousness. You are not worried about the future and you don´t regret what you did in the past. You are not thinking about what happened yesterday or three weeks ago, what you might cook for dinner, what your colleagues said this morning, who you are going to call next. You are just right here, right now, in this present moment; nothing more.

. The word "sanzen" literally means "three-thousand" which stands for everything that possibly exists in this world. I got it.

> *Ichinen-sanzen* means: being fully tuned into this present moment, my heart is connected to abundant and rich possibilities in the universe. That´s when I can choose and unfold a new reality.

In this present moment I had all the possibilities in me. That´s why I had a choice. You reach this state of mind when you deeply focus on the Gohonzon and become one with it whilst chanting. In deep concentration and awareness, in the here and now, I was connected to everything and therefore I could influence everything. Everything was in me and I was everything. That´s why I could influence everything whilst chanting. Therefore, change *always* occurs from the inside, spreading to the outside. But what did I have to consider?

> Change always occurs from the inside to the outside. You can change in this one single moment.

Let´s go through this again. Ichinen, related to the holistic philosophy of ichinen-sanzen, means one concentrated state of mind, or "one heart at this present moment". Since all possibilities (sanzen) are contained in this state of focused awareness (ichinen), change can emerge from it. Since in this state of mind I am connected to everything, I can influence everything. Ichinen might therefore also be understood in the sense of determination, visualization or intention, but in a deeper sense it always means a concentrated state of mind beyond our everyday consciousness. Therefore the word "ichinen" can be understood as "an intention deep from the heart in this present moment." This type of determination and intention is in connection with something greater than ourselves. Thus we do not fight with our own will or our own personal skills alone, but in cooperation with **daimoku.**

Ichinen does not mean your own will at the level of your everyday ego, but your own intention in connection with your higher self.

Your higher self carries your intention and we assume the lead in so far as we provide it with our goals and ideas. Therefore, the exact construction and formulation of the desired target is very important, since our higher self is a neutral observer that will lead us to our goals.

We need a constant, clear visualization of the desired state as well as access to our higher self. This access, however, is not on the level of everyday consciousness. As long as we only act with our own will at the level of our ego as part of our everyday consciousness and "decide" something, we only act on our own will power, not at the level of our highest self. Once again it was the description of Anita Moorjani's near-death experience that offered a vivid example of the fact that ichinen-sanzen was not a theoretical concept but a phenomenon that can be experienced.

She experienced her higher self as a state of perfect oneness and interpenetration with universal life energy. *"During my near death experience there was nothing outside of my broader awareness because I was one with the totality of universal energy. It felt as if I included totality. In this state there was absolute clarity and everything was available to this knowledge. I seemed to be everything and I existed in everything."*

> *"The fact that I could see my own greatness and realize that the universe and I were one, was the reason for my healing."* (Anita Moorjani)

Anita Moorjani experienced the principle of ichinen-sanzen by realizing that she herself was "the whole" in the sense that we ourselves are one with universal energy. But we ourselves, our analytical mind and our restricted view often block this connection with universal life energy. *"I found that a view directed from the inside to the outside means that I trust my inner guidance completely. It is as if what I feel has an effect on the whole universe. In other words, the whole gets influenced by me because I am in the center of my cosmic web. As far as I am concerned, the universe is happy as long as I am happy. If I love myself, everybody else will love me, too. When I am at peace with myself, the whole of creation is at peace with itself."*

You are carried by the power of daimoku

Everything Anita Moorjani was feeling had an impact on the whole and, the very moment she felt the oneness with universal life energy, her healing at this level of consciousness began to happen. Therefore, the principle of ichinen-sanzen means the unfolding of our higher self in the depth of life. Then we are carried by the flow of life force energy and the solutions come to our life. We don't have to look outside for solutions.

This was my experience years ago, when after a very disappointing experience I suddenly had severe back problems. Someone I thought I could trust visited me at home and attacked me verbally in a very unpleasant way. She metaphorically "stabbed me in the back" without warning, but I never thought my body would feel this physically as well. After this disappointing experience, I had lumbago that caused constant pain down my right leg. I tried any medical or alternative treatment I could find, but nothing helped. The only option I had was to take a tablet against the pain once in a while, which I tried not to do because these tablets had many side effects and could lead to stomach ulcers. After two years I had really tried everything and I came to a point where I could only chant deeply that the pain would go away, and where I gave the matter over to the Gohonzon.

At that time my husband Yukio had been sent to Shanghai by his company for a couple of months. I flew to Shanghai in order to be with him. I was afraid of the flight, as it was very difficult with my back pain to sit for twelve hours. However, I wanted to take the opportunity to try Chinese acupuncture. The Chinese secretary of my husband´s company arranged an appointment with a practitioner of Chinese medicine. I'd only had a curiosity, but it "accidentally" turned out that the doctor was an absolute specialist in spinal and back problems and had previously been successful servicing the Japanese Osaka football team. He went with his hands along my spine and within two minutes he had recognized the reason for my two-year pain.

My spine had shifted and with a special treatment of tuina massage to straighten my spine, the whole problem was resolved. Only eight treatments later I was free of pain. After one of the treatments caused a decisive advance, I wondered why that afternoon I felt emotionally very bad. Suddenly I felt exactly the feeling I had that day when this woman, whom I had trusted so much, directly attacked me verbally whilst visiting me at home and metaphorically "stabbed me in the back".

Why was it that there in China I intensely re-experienced a feeling I had two years ago? That´s when I understood: all this time this feeling had been stored in my body and was now being released again as the original status was being restored to my spine. At that moment I recognized the deep connection between my back pain and this long past event. I was deeply grateful and recognized that, after two years of trying to find an appropriate treatment using my own strategy, my strong **daimoku** and the handing over of this problem to the Gohonzon led exactly to this physician who could resolve my problems. I found it very "mystic"!

Chapter 4
The Ceremony in the Air

Why did Nichiren inscribe the Gohonzon?

Why it is not enough to only recite the mantra of Nam-myō-hō-ren-ge-kyō without focusing on a Gohonzon (mandala)? One could also recite daimoku without a Gohonzon, so what was the difference? Ultimately this question boiled down why Nichiren had inscribed the Gohonzon and what this actually meant. Nichiren had recited Nam-myō-hō-ren-ge-kyō for the first time at Seichōji-temple. At that time he had not said a single word about a mandala, let alone about inscribing one. What had caused him to do so later on the island of Sado?

I'd had many experiences with the practice of daimoku and I knew that it worked. Why then was it that Nichiren himself had so many problems? Why did he not live a comfortable, wealthy, prosperous, peaceful and calm life? The answer to this question was given to me on a small island in the Sea of Japan.

On our way to Sado

In Japan we had seen and visited all the key sites of Nichiren´s life and work. There was one place yet to see, the place where he had produced his first Mandala-Gohonzon and his most important writings: on the island of Sado. After the failed attempt to decapitate Nichiren at Tatsunokuchi, he was banished to an extremely cold and dangerous island from which no exile had ever come back alive again. This island is under the heavy influence of Siberia´s cold. But Nichiren survived even that. What was it like there? I wanted to know.

In April 2013 we finally found the time and the opportunity to drive to Teradomari, the port city of the Sea of Japan, where Nichiren had been waiting for his crossing to the island of Sado. We arrived during a raging storm. The whole night thunderous,

Sado in winter

powerful waves and torrential rain hit against the window and kept us awake. At the same time there was an icy wind blowing that made us feel the approaching cold from Siberia.

There I was, in my safe and dry hotel room on my futon – but how must Nichiren have felt when he had been waiting at that location for six days on his passage through this monster-sea? Furthermore, he was not a tourist but was sent as a criminal.

I could not stand the wind and the rain for more than a minute without being thrown back and forth physically. We crossed this dangerous sea to Sado on a large, safe ferry which protected us from the threatening, thrashing waves. But Nichiren? How did he manage in a small, wooden boat?

Car ferry to Sado

The first station: a place of horror

Our first stop on the island had also been Nichiren's in November 1271: Tsukahara, the place where the dead bodies of the island's inhabitants were stored. Today there is a small temple at exactly the place where there had once been a tiny, rotten shack called *Tsukahara Sanmaido*. It was not just the icy cold and the hunger that troubled him. Followers of other Buddhist schools were lingering everywhere, waiting to kill him for daring to criticize them. Now he had come, exposed to that bitterly cold hell and surrounded by the discarded corpses of the deceased islanders. In this lonely and threatening situation Nichiren felt as if he had, as he wrote: "*I felt as though I had passed through the realm of hungry spirits and fallen alive into one of the cold hells*" (»Letter to Hōren« of 1275).

Would he survive this winter? It is hard to imagine that he was still able to think about anything besides this one question. But even so, he managed the unimaginable. Firstly, Nichiren managed to win the heart of a lay monk named Abutsubō,

Tsukahara Sanmaidō

who had wanted to kill him, in such a profound way that he started to practice daimoku. Later Abutsubō even helped Nichiren, for he and his wife regularly procured food for Nichiren. Secondly, in February 1272 and under the worst conditions, Nichiren managed to write one of his main works, "The Opening of the Eyes", which he later described as "his will": "*On the twelfth day of the ninth month of last year, between the hours of the rat and the ox (11:00 P.M. to 3:00 A.M.), this person named Nichiren was beheaded. It is his soul that has come to this island of Sado and, in the second month of the following year, snowbound, is writing this to send to his close disciples. ... It may also be regarded as a keepsake from me"* (»The Opening of the Eyes« of 1272).

In it he revealed his true identity as Jōgyō, the leader of the Bodhisattvas from the Earth, who according to the description of the Lotus Sutra would proclaim the dharma of the Lotus Sutra after the death of Buddha Shakyamuni.

The second station: a place of enlightenment

Later Nichiren was moved to Ichinosawa, where he could lead a relatively quiet and secure life under the protection of an officer. In his capacity as Bodhisattva *Jōgyō* – as a spiritual, enlightened being who was deeply connected to the cosmic consciousness of the universe – Nichiren wrote his other main work in April 1273, »The Treaty on the Object of Devotion for Observing One´s Heart (*Kanjin-no-honzon-shō*)«. In it he describes the content and structure of the mandala in detail. Three months later, he inscribed the first Mandala-Gohonzon, equipped with the Ten Worlds as it is known today in its basic form.

After having arrived at Ichinosawa, I was filled with deep awe. Here was the place where Nichiren finished what he had begun in Kominato on the mountain of Seichōji-temple. Seichōji was the birthplace of **daimoku**, where Nichiren first recited **Nam-myō-hō-ren-ge-kyō** to the rising sun; here in Ichinosawa he had inscribed a Mandala-Gohonzon for the first time. Why had he not done this beforehand, why not even then in Seichōji?

The answer lay in all the stages of Nichiren´s life we had visited previously and which were a testimony to the fact that Nichiren had overcome all persecution. And there was a lot of persecution. The first attack he survived was when his cottage was assaulted by

In front of the first mandala-gohonzon,
inscribed on July 8, 1273 (copy)

a hostile group of Buddhist monks in Matsubagayatsu. Then he was attacked and even wounded by a group of soldiers in Komatsubara. Afterwards they tried to kill him by exposing him on a rock in the sea of the Island of Izu. Later there was an attempt to decapitate him in Tatsunokuchi. Nothing had worked so far. Now he was send to exile on Sado. He overcame even this life-threatening situation.

Once my husband´s cousin, who himself is a very convinced Nichiren Buddhist, asked me why exactly I was so fascinated about Nichiren despite the fact that I had originally been brought up in a Christian country. Considering this question I realized why: *You could not kill him!* Moreover, Nichiren was the only Buddhist master who I really felt had a respectful attitude towards women. He considered them not only as absolutely "equivalent" to men but also as "venerable and deserving gratitude" because women give birth to and raise children.

Before inscribing the Gohonson, Nichiren himself first needed to prove that what was said in the Lotus Sutra was true, because he was reading it as a prophecy for his own appearance in this world.

The Lotus Sutra states above all that 2,000 years after Shakya-muni's death (according to the old calendar) there would appear someone who would teach the Lotus Sutra and suffer significant slander and persecution. Nichiren fulfilled this prophecy and proved himself to be "the practitioner of the Lotus Sutra". In particular, however, Nichiren saw himself as the reincarnation of Bodhisattva Jōgyō, the leader of the Bodhisattvas of the Earth, who were entrusted by Buddha Shakyamuni with the mission to proclaim the Mystic Law.

But why weren't the other great Bodhisattvas like Avalo-kiteshvara and Maitreya not entrusted with this mission? This was one of the central questions that was raised and answered in the Ceremony in the Air. It was revealed that only the Bodhisattvas of the Earth were the direct disciples of the original Buddha and incorporated the same *Mystic Law* (*Myōhō*) that enabled the original Buddha, the origin of all Buddhas in the universe, to attain enlightenment in the eternal past. This means that both the original Buddha and the Bodhisattvas of the Earth embody the Mystic Law and, thus, the state of enlightenment within themselves.

Therefore, in the capacity as the reincarnation of Bodhisattva Jōgyō, Nichiren was now able to inscribe the Mandala-Gohonzon of the Mystic Law. Thus, when you chant **daimoku** in front of the Gohonzon, you have direct access to your enlightened state manifested in the Gohonzon. That means you can activate your enlightened state immediately in order to create a fulfilled and happy life.

I now understood that I owe this wonderful possibility to Nichiren, because he dedicated his whole life to overcoming so many difficulties in order to establish the practice of the great Mystic Law. As he declares, I can equally prove to be a Bodhisattva of the Earth when I chant **daimoku** in front of this Gohonzon.

> Nichiren needed a proof to be the reincarnation
> of Bodhisattva Jōgyō who was entitled to manifest
> the eternal Mystic Law of Nam-myō-hō-ren-ge-kyō
> in the Gohonzon.

Believe in Nichiren's mandala

Now I understood why Nichiren had not inscribed the Gohonzon
before Sado, and why practicing to the Gohonzon was the central
aspect of his teachings. In Ichinosawa I saw the first "Ten World
Mandala Gohonzon" that Nichiren had ever inscribed. I was deeply moved: How many people in the world today recite daimoku to
a Gohonzon and have amazing and life-changing experiences with
it? Here was the original and first version of such a mandala. I had
arrived at the source. This source was crystal clear and clean.

At first Nichiren only spoke about having faith in the Lotus Sutra,
but after he had inscribed the Gohonzon, he spoke about having
faith in the Gohonzon. From now on, this aspect became essential
for the practice of reciting daimoku. This becomes clear in Nichiren's letter to his follower Shijō Kingo and his wife, written only a
few weeks after he
had inscribed the
first Gohonzon in
August 1273. Thus,
Shijō Kingo was one
of the first people
ever who experi-
enced the effect of
the Gohonzon.
Nichiren wrote to
him after he had
learned that the
little daughter of

*The house of Shijō Kingo used to be
located on this ground in Kamakura*

Shijō Kingo was seriously ill. In this letter he asks Shijō Kingo to fully trust the mandala that he had sent him for his protection. Literally he wrote: *"The lion king is said to advance three steps, then gather himself to spring, unleashing the same power whether he traps a tiny ant or attacks a fierce animal. In inscribing this Gohonzon for her protection, Nichiren was like the lion king. (...) Believe in this mandala with all your heart. Nam-myō-hō-ren-ge-kyō is like the roar of a lion. What sickness can therefore be an obstacle?"* (»Reply to Kyō'ō« of 1273).

What happened next? Well, Shijō Kingo followed the advice of Nichiren and was one of the first who experienced the healing power of practicing to the Gohonzon. His daughter became completely healthy again.

Nichiren´s mandala

Nichiren himself stated that he had inscribed all the "states of life" in this mandala that both exist in the universe and in the life of an individual person. These are known in Nichiren Buddhism as the Ten Worlds, or the "ten states of life ranging from hell up to the state of Buddhahood". In this process both the universe and the individual human being and his or her environment go through constantly changing conditions. This aspect was exemplified by Nichiren to his loyal female follower Nichinyo when he explained that all kinds of life of the universe are represented in the Gohonzon, but that due to the practice of **daimoku** they show their "enlightened nature". That means as long as the practice of **daimoku** is the center of my life, negative life conditions cannot dominate me and will be transformed into something positive.

I found this fascinating and something I could actually experience myself. Thus, Nichiren´s mandala contains the entire cosmos including all its various energy states. The **daimoku** of "Nam-myō-hō-ren-ge-kyō" in the middle represents the universal life energy that is the source of all appearances and phenomena in the universe. Better yet, by chanting **daimoku** in front of this mandala everybody has the immediate opportunity to align to this highest energetic state and thus come into harmony with it.

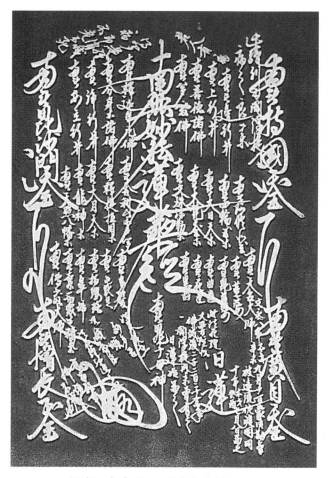

Nichiren's first mandala in Ichinosawa

So I did not need to have a near-death experience, as Anita Moorjani had described it, in order to come into harmony with this universal life energy. Nichiren´s mandala already contained the energetic signature of this state. I just had to align to it. Now I understood why Nichiren´s first mandala contained the addition: "*Those who believe in this sutra will be cured of any disease*". In this case the mandala itself represents the enlightened cosmic dimension and is available to us so that we can enter this sacred, mystical world. Nichiren had always stressed that this was the central point of his teaching and practice. In a further letter to his follower Nichinyo he even described the Gohonzon as a "treasure tower" to which you have access by absolutely believing in it. But what exactly did Nichiren mean by this?

The Ceremony in the Air

Beyond the individual energetic life-states, Nichiren´s mandala contains a further deep meaning, the scope and depth of which I only grasped gradually. In his treatise about the Gohonzon, Nichiren himself described in detail that the mandala represents a particular scene from the Lotus Sutra called the *Ceremony in the Air*. Nichiren said that every time we chant **daimoku** to the Gohonzon, we participate in this ceremony. What did he mean by this? Did this mean that the Gohonzon was a projection of this ceremony described in the Lotus Sutra? But what did this ceremony stand for and why did it occur *in the air*?

The scene depicted in the Lotus Sutra represents a meeting with the historical Buddha Shakyamuni, in which the Lotus Sutra is proclaimed. It first takes place on the earthly, material level (on Eagle Peak). After Buddha Shakyamuni stressed the great benefits that can be obtained through the practice of the Lotus Sutra, a magnificent, oversized treasure tower decorated with jewels emerged from the earth and floated into the air. The participants in this meeting were also lifted up in the air with the help of the supernatural powers of the Buddha.

In the air? I did some research and found out that this is also a *
metaphor for *a level beyond time and space*. In the end the only
participants left in the Ceremony in the Air were those who
sincerely believed in the Lotus Sutra. Thus, there is one require-
ment to meet this level: absolute confidence in the Buddhist law *
expressed in the Lotus Sutra. This means that only by completely
letting go and by entirely trusting, relying and opening up to the
Gohonzon can one reach this level. Shakyamuni opened the door
to the treasure tower and in it was sitting a Buddha called *Taho* *
("many treasures") who offered for Shakyamuni to take the place
next to him.

In this form the great visionary scene is depicted, the "Cere- *
mony in the Air", which begins with the ascending of the treasure
tower in the Lotus Sutra's 11th chapter and ends in the 22nd
chapter, when the task of preaching and spreading the dharma of
the Lotus Sutra after Shakyamuni's death was transferred to the
Bodhisattvas. After that, all participants returned to the earthly
world, where many Bodhisattvas who bear such illustrious names
as Medicine King, Wonderful Sound or Universal Wisdom,
developed their wonderful activities for the benefit of the people.

A wall painting of the „Ceremony in the Air"
in the Mogao-Grottoes from the 8th Century, Dunhuang, China

Chapter 5
A World Full of Energy and Possibilities

Emptiness in quantum physics

Only by an excursion into the world of quantum physics did I begin to comprehend the true, profound significance of this symbolically depicted "Ceremony in the Air." Suddenly everything fell into place. In quantum physics there is also talk of a dimension *beyond time and space*. I was fascinated.

Could it be that the Buddhist masters of earlier times, in particular Nichiren, had already realized things that scientists can only confirm today? The research field of quantum physics has existed for almost a hundred years now, but the results of this new way to look at reality have not really penetrated social consciousness. This research looks beyond the perceptible and material and tries to fathom the reality behind the appearances of the outer world. Quantum physicists also say that the nature of things is "empty"; they even go so far as to claim that matter itself does not actually exist. Instead, research showed that there might be a kind of "life energy" or "life force" that penetrates the whole universe and everything and every living being, and which connects us to everything and to each other.

In order to depict the fantastic scenery of the Ceremony in the Air, Buddhist masters must have experienced the great vision of an unlimited sphere not only in the universe but also within themselves.

The physicists discuss the existence of a "quantum field", a "universal intelligence" or an invisible field of information, a dimension of infinite possibilities that exists *beyond time and space* and which is supposed to be the source of all material phenomena and all experiences. This quantum field consists of information and energy and, at its deepest level, of only pure consciousness.

In this information field all possible experiences exist as potentialities not yet realized. That´s why the scientists talk about an "unlimited field of possibilities" or the "sea of all possibilities". This gives an idea of what the treasure tower in the Ceremony in the Air symbolically stands for. But before we delve into the quantum universe, let's first have a look at where our idea of reality, as we know it so far, actually comes from.

The idea of a reality separated from us

Are we not brought up with the idea that the things that happen around us exist independently of us? And do we not often have the feeling that we do not have any control over them? In a sense it's like a movie that is already filmed − but we ourselves aren´t the director of it. When I am abruptly cut off in traffic by another driver, then it is not me who actually caused this situation - or is it?

It´s definitely not my "fault" that other people behave the way they do, or does it have to do something with my own life deep down? If I am surrounded by a domineering boss and permanently grumpy colleagues, then this has got nothing to do with me - or does it? Many of you will think "no", that I might be able to change my attitude towards my environment, but I don´t have any direct influence on my environment.

> We believe that external reality is
> independent of our thoughts and feelings.

But what is at the deepest level behind this reality? Is reality not how it was taught to us? What is the true nature of reality? Can we possibly affect it?

The problematic separation of body and mind

How did we actually get the idea that everything around us runs •
without our intervention, almost like a machine that runs on its
own program? We owe this kind of thinking to the classical
sciences, for due to René Descartes and Sir Isaac Newton the
consideration of reality was divided into two categories in the 17th
century: into mind and matter.

These two areas were neatly separated and the study of matter
and the material world was left to the natural sciences, because it
was assumed that the objective outer world was predictable and
separated from one's own inner experience. The world of spirit
and of one's inner experience was from now on the topic of
religion and of the humanities.

Thus spirit and matter were increasingly separated and   •
considered to be two completely different and
independent units.

Through this separation we have all more or less unconsciously ▪
internalized the idea that we live in a material, physical world and
that the *reality out there* is independent of our consciousness and
of our emotional state. As a matter of fact, we do not have any
influence on the orbits of the countless planets in the universe or
on the cycles of the four seasons on earth, which provide a number of general conditions in our lives. That's why most people still
consider the world of matter to be the only reality that they
perceive with their five senses and which they can clearly grasp
with their mind. The material world appears to be solid, meas- ▪
urable, predictable and largely explained mechanically, therefore

you can predict, based on the calculated data, which orbits the planets draw around the sun and how long a flight takes from Frankfurt to Tokyo. In classical physics the whole universe appears to work as precisely as a clock. We take that as real what we perceive. That´s *reality, isn´t it?*

Orbits of the planets

So far, such questions were no problem in the classical sciences, according to which we consider all life as human beings, animals and plants as material things upon which our consciousness has no influence. We have completely lost the knowledge of spiritual and energetic influences on our lives out of sight, because we have internalized a materialistic and mechanistic understanding of reality. As long as we adhere to a material concept of reality, the true nature of reality remains hidden to us. We miss the opportunity to change our own reality according to our individual ideas.

More than 750 years ago, Nichiren seems to have lived in a completely different world, where everything was inspired by living energies and where everything was deeply connected. He describes, for example, that often he directly communicated with the universe, talking to the shining stars and the lightning moon in the darkness in Tsukahara: *"In the yard around the hut the snow piled deeper and deeper. No one came to see me; my only visitor was the piercing wind. Tendai's Great Meditation and the Lotus Sutra lay open before my eyes, and Nam-myō-hō-ren-ge-kyō flowed from my lips. My evenings passed in discourse to the moon and stars on the fallacies of the various schools and the profound*

meaning of the Lotus Sutra. Thus, one year gave way to the next"
(»The Actions of the Votary of the Lotus Sutra« of 1276).

I think we should take this statement of Nichiren very seriously. Just imagine the following scenario. It is a winter evening and you are sitting in a hut in a wild field without heating, electricity, radio or TV. You are gazing at the sky that is full of brilliantly shining stars. You are a part of the fascinating and unlimited universe. How do you feel? This is the spiritual dimension Nichiren must have experienced all the time.

For this reason, the power of daimoku was probably much more ·
real to him than the purely material world. He drew his strength
and energy from another level of reality. For him, the influence of
spiritual energies was absolutely real and almost eight hundred
years later, it is now possible to make the secret of this other level
visible – thanks to modern physics.

The energetic worldview of quantum physics

Since the last century the findings of quantum physics have led to
a completely new world view that turns our conception of reality
upside down. We are in the process of a massive paradigm shift.

The central message of quantum physical research in the last ·
century is that just below the surface of our everyday life, when
we leave the visible and experiential level, there is a different,

mysterious world that does not penetrate our consciousness immediately.

The German quantum physicist Ulrich Warnke calls this world the "inter-world" and thinks it to be "more real" than our everyday world, since he considers it to be the actual reality compared to perceived reality. Interestingly enough, this is also what people report who have made mystical experiences. Behind the visible, tangible world there are several levels of reality. The deeper one penetrates into matter, the more it dissolves. The question is, how deep do you want to penetrate into this mystery?

The floor under your feet ... does not exist

Before I get up every morning I certainly believe that there is a floor when I swing myself out of bed, regardless of what I thought or dreamt the night before. Or have you ever experienced that there was no floor when you woke up in the morning? Well then, what is "real" and what do we think is "real"?

Classical physics comes to its limits when studying the smallest building blocks of our visible material world: the atoms, which are the building blocks of the entire physical universe. The more quantum physicists disassembled the atom in its smallest components, the more it dissolved. According to quantum physics, at a deeper level even the solid material things that surround us seem to dissolve "in its deepest core". The scientists wanted to find out what atoms really exist of. The result was astonishing.

For they found that they do not contain any solid components any more, as we know from the past from our physics lessons long time ago. The researchers came to the conclusion that the basic, most elementary level of matter is "empty", mostly immaterial. The modern physicists were literally left with nothing. With nothing?

Old and new model of the atom

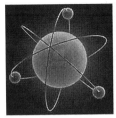

Do you still remember the picture of an atom which was portrayed to us at physics at school? Before quantum physics an atom looked like a billiard ball, which represents the solid core, and which is surrounded by electrons. In this case we are mainly dealing with material things, with matter. Classical physics assumed that matter consists of atoms which were regarded as the supposedly solid building blocks of the material universe. Thus atoms were portrayed as small solid billiard balls that orbit each other and which consist of a core which is surrounded by electrons which move around the nucleus.

The closer the quantum physicists looked at the smallest components of the atom, however, the less outlined it became, until it almost disappeared. They found that atoms consist of 99.99999% of empty space. This *empty* space, however, is *not at all empty* – it consists of energy and information.

Only 0.00001 percent of the atom consists of matter.
Materially speaking, it is practically nothing,
but potentially it is everything.

All matter is therefore more energy than solid. Instead of thinking in terms of *things* one might therefore rather think of *options*. The things that feel solid for us are therefore actually energy, apart from a tiny little bit of matter.

The famous quantum physicist Max Planck declared that actually matter does not really exist (at the subatomic level), but that all things ultimately are only energy fields that manifest as vibration. Everything consists only of vibration? How can we imagine that everything is empty space?

Now, assume for a moment that the nucleus of an atom would be as big as a football, then the electron surrounding it would be about 30 kilometers away and the entire space between them would be *empty*. But that does not mean that there is "nothing". Quite the contrary. It just means that what fills up this room is not material. Because this seemingly matter-free space is not completely empty but contains an enormous amount of non-tangible *energy and information.* So what about the "empty space" in which the Ceremony in the Air takes place?

> The "empty space" in which the Ceremony in the Air
> takes place can also be described as a place full of
> energy and information of abundant and rich possibilities,
> for which the "treasure tower" is also a symbol for.
> Once we have access to this level,
> we become creators of our own reality.

And what about us human beings? A mathematician has calculated that the "pure matter" of a seven-foot man, i.e. if you omit the entire "nothing" of "empty space", could be reduced to a two millimeter cookie – quite frustrating for many a bodybuilder who has made so much effort to inflate his body only to find out that behind it is "almost nothing". What really brings life to our bodies is a form of energy, namely the same 99.99999% "nothing" or energy that represent almost the entirety of the physical universe. So why is it then that again and again we only focus on the 0.00001% of reality that is actually physical?

Each atom is therefore more energy than matter and is surrounded by a certain energetic field. When two or more atoms come together, they combine to form molecules and correspondingly larger energy fields arise. Anything material in this world

consists almost entirely of non-matter, but rather of energy fields
and frequency patterns of information. If we want to change
something, then we need access to this energy field of information. *STRINGS AND MEMBRANES*

Our cells communicate together through sounds

The cell researchers James Gimzewski and Andrew Pelling from
the University of California in Los Angeles found out that even our
body cells are dynamic units that move and produce vibrations
that can be perceived as sounds. They found out, for example, that

yeast cells communicate
with each other in tones
as the high C or D,
whereas alcohol literally
causes cells to "scream".
Cancer cells, however,
emit sounds that sound
more like noise. However, this applies only to living cells, because
dead cells only just emit a low, deep murmur.

With these findings the researchers hope that, in future,
diseases can be "heard" and that they will be able to discover
diseases in advance before they break out. Well, in the meantime
we know that the entire universe consists of vibration. Even the
mantra Nam-myō-hō-ren-ge-kyō has a special vibrational pattern. By
pronouncing it loudly it unfolds its inherent effect.

Nam-myō-hō-ren-ge-kyō is vibration.
When we chant, we change the vibration of our cells.

We are energetic beings

In order to exist in our three-dimensional reality of everyday life, we consist of bones, muscles, blood and organs. Here we are a tangible body and subject to the laws of gravity and here we have our everyday experiences. If a piano falls on our foot in the midst of moving to another apartment, then we do not doubt the existence of matter or the effect of gravity in the least.

The world of quantum mechanics appears when one penetrates deeper into the molecules and atoms and further immerses into the subatomic world. There we are virtually in a matter-free space, where the atoms dissolve and become energy and information. Our bodies also consist of organized energy and information fields that are associated with the unifying quantum field.

One could say that at a quantum level we are all part of a huge "energy soup" and that all objects – every living being and every object in the physical functional area- is nothing more than an energetic accumulation floating in this energy soup. On the quantum level we become one energetic system where everything is connected to everything. We live in an energetic system of unity and connectedness, full of pulsating energy fields in a single gigantic energy field. Sometimes we feel this embeddedness. We feel the energy of places that mixes with our own energy: when we enter a calm, clear place like a meditation room or a church, or when we enter a room where there is "thick air" or where there is a fun atmosphere. We also feel the individual energy field of another person, in what mood he or she is, what kind of emotions he or she emits, and how we are touched and influenced by them.

Emotions are highly "contagious"; therefore,
who we surround ourselves with is very important,
because people can influence our energy field
in either a positive or a negative way.

Life is energy. You are energy. Your partner is energy. Your thoughts are energy. Your emotions are energy. At the core that is each of us really is: energy. On a deeper level there are obviously no boundaries between us and all other things in our environment. Despite the appearance that we are separate, once we are near  other people, our energy fields touch each other, merge with each other and disengage from each other again. In this process we constantly exchange energy and information. Every time we meet, however, we lose a small part of our energy field to the other person and in exchange receive a small part of the energy field of this person. Therefore, every encounter changes our energy a little bit.

> Other people cannot escape our vibrational field
> when they resonate with us. Our energy causes
> other people to vibrate accordingly.
> We make other people vibrate by our own energy.

It is important to be conscious of your own energy. Your personal energy is sending out vibrations into the quantum field. Others will entrain to your frequency. Your energy impacts your relationships and you have to keep your energy field clean. My husband and I felt this phenomenon increasingly intensively, the more we "cleaned" our energy field by practicing daimoku. Suddenly we experienced a strange phenomenon.

Whilst in Japan we met one of our German friends for dinner. We had not seen him for a very long time, but in the meantime his energy field had become very obscured by too much alcohol and by his constant negative, pessimistic and depressive moods, which he had developed due to business failures and personal disappointments. He felt trapped and actually did not see any sense in his life any more. We spent an entire evening with him in a sushi restaurant and were surprised that the next day we felt very bad both physically and mentally.

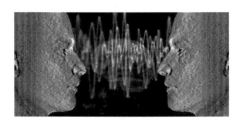

Deep down we both felt this dark state of life without hope. It was almost as if we had shared the painful state of hell with him. Without realizing it, we had both experienced that we had been "pulled down" by our friend´s energy field in the truest sense of the word.

To change therefore means to change your own energy.

When you spend time with somebody and you share your ideas with that person, you invite his or her energy into your energy field. You can easily tell if somebody is bringing positive energy or dissonance into your field. When someone is bringing harmony to your field, then there is supportive energy that makes you feel inspired and energetic after speaking with them. Your energetic field feels much stronger. When someone is bringing dissonance to your energetic field, then you feel energetically drained after speaking with that person. Suddenly you feel less excited about the ideas you shared with them. When you are not aware of this possibility, you can unconsciously come into sync with the lower vibrational emotions others carry with them. This in turn might cause energetic holes in your own energetic field. As we can see in later chapters of this book, we are really talking about "holes" or "blockages" in our energetic field. They occur when we are stressed out or experiencing a negative emotion.

Exercise 5

Do you sometimes feel energetically drained by certain people or circumstances in your life? Can you identify them?

- -

- -

What kind of energy do we send to other people?

Since there is a constant exchange of energy and information between people, animals, plants and with our environment, it is very important to be aware of what kind of energy we send out to other people. If a person in our environment feels bad, then we can "send" the positive energy of the daimoku to this person. We don´t even need to be close to this person, because the daimoku is transmitted at a level beyond time and space and the concept of room does not exist for us in this respect, as we already realized.

Just imagine this person was in front of you and visualize him or her in your mind. Now "radiate" towards this person, so to say, with daimoku. However, in doing so you should try to feel as good as possible yourself and try not to think negatively about the status of this person. "Compassionate" thoughts that see the other person as "a poor person who feels so bad" represent an energy that might only amplify the negative state of the other person. Therefore, it is better to visualize with all clarity whilst chanting that the other person is already healthy and happy again and has overcome his or her current situation. Even if the other person cannot become healthy again, the energy you send out whilst chanting daimoku may also be a great relief for that person.

In 1998 my aunt was diagnosed with stomach cancer. Over the course of the following year, I saw her physical body diminish. The time came she had to stay in hospital and, step by step, her condition became worse. The night before she passed I stayed with her in her hospital room. As I sat by her bedside, she was mostly unconscious but she was also in deep pain. I could tell because she was constantly groaning and lashing around with her arms. Her eyes were rolling in her head and she was still fighting to stay in this world. I´m not sure if she was aware that I was in the room. I did not know how to help her, so I put my portable Gohonzon on the table and started to chant **daimoku**, hoping that she could hear me. Suddenly she stopped lashing around with her arms and became very calm. As I continued to chant I could feel her energy releasing weight and she had a relaxed expression on her face. Every time I stopped chanting that night, she would start groaning in pain and lashing with her arms again. Every time I resumed chanting, she would immediately become calm and stop groaning. I chanted as much as I could that night and I truly began to understand the power of **daimoku**.

Chapter 6
From Matter to Energy

The second paradigm shift: from matter to energy

Do you still remember the first chapter and how we broadly identify ourselves with our limited everyday ego consciousness? Does that mean that our problems are caused by the fact that we are not aware of our true identity? We have a great and limitless higher self which is in connection with the enlightened cosmic consciousness. In order to understand the importance of unfolding and activating your own higher self, which is often referred to as our own "Buddha nature," it is necessary to apply a new paradigm not only of one's self and one's own identity, but of the entire universe and the nature of reality. You cannot pour new wine into old wineskins – this higher self cannot live only in the limited world of a materialistic and mechanistic world view.

What deeply fascinated me about the practice of Nichiren Buddhism right from the beginning was its claim to be able to change your own reality. This claim goes back to the Lotus Sutra. Doesn't it say that disease and poverty can be overcome and that you can become happy in this life by exercising this sutra? Didn't Nichiren already encourage Shijō Kingo to chant so intensively and determined like a roaring lion for his daughter to recover from her illness?

Shijō Kingo had been successful in this respect. Doesn't that mean that one's own reality can be changed and that a change in one's own consciousness may even cause another person's physical state to change? Interestingly enough, Shijō Kingo, who himself was a medical doctor, tried his best to heal his daughter on the physical level, but in the end managed to heal her on another level of reality: on the level of enlightened consciousness.

But are we not conditioned to always look on the outside first to find a solution? Could reality be influenced by our own state of consciousness? Let's take a look at this, going one step deeper into the nature of reality as it is described by the latest findings of quantum physics and by Nichiren himself.

When we practice Nichiren Buddhism, then we make a paradigm shift - away from our deep-rooted belief that *the solution lies solely in the fact that external conditions and circumstances change* to the statement of Nichiren: *Never seek this Gohonzon outside yourself.* But what exactly does this mean? Interestingly, Nichiren is backed up by the results of recent studies of new scientific approaches that are now trying to integrate consciousness and energy. Does his statement mean that on a certain level of consciousness we can influence external reality? Let's have a look at the conclusions some quantum physicists have come to.

Famous author and neuroscientist Joe Dispenza gives us a very deep and extriguing insight into such a new "quantum model of reality", as he calls it. In the following paragraphs you will find a more detailied explanation of the core principles he attributes to such a new way of looking not just at reality but also at life.

Reality, as we know it, is in fact more complex and richer than we are aware of.

A quantum field of possibilities

Hopefully by now you have become fascinated by the basic concepts of the quantum model. Let's sum up again: The entire physical reality is primarily energy. Quantum physics asserts that there is a level of existence beyond the visible, tangible world that is no longer material, but of energetic nature and which is called the quantum level, quantum field or energy field. We are all part of this huge, invisible energy field that connects all people, things and beings with each other and moreover contains all events and states as information that have not yet materialized. Therefore, this energy field is called the "sea of all possibilities."

This is where everything exists as a potential.

The quantum field is invisible, potential energy that always continues to lower in frequency until it reorganizes itself via particles, molecules and atoms into matter. Matter forms all physical things, for instance, a human body. Like everything in the universe, we are connected to this sea of information in the universe that exists beyond physical ("Einsteinian") space and time.

The scientific journalist Lynne McTaggart describes in detail that quantum processes can also take place between people, since we are all connected in one energy field together. This may explain 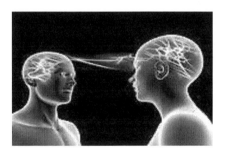 phenomena such as telepathy and premonitions, e.g. when someone calls us. Recently this just happened to me: I was just thinking about a female friend who lives in Thailand and I was wondering how she was doing, and just that second the phone rang. I was almost frightened: it was as if we had been communicating all along on an invisible level. This phenomenon can be explained by presuming that we are all connected with each other in an energetic field.

With the concept of telepathy we often think of a sender and a receiver: the sender sends his or her thoughts and transmits them to another person. This idea, however, is linear and cannot explain the phenomenon of telepathy over a distance of thousands of kilometers within the terms of classical physics. At the energy field level this phenomenon can be easily explained. In this case, sender and receiver are basically part of one field, where information is exchangeable and readable.

We do not live in a "solid" reality. The underlying reality of our material world is one big energy field that penetrates everybody and everything. The whole time I had been connected to my friend via this energetic field, no matter where she was. Most people have experienced such energetic phenomena. Sometimes this is the phone that is ringing and you know who is calling. Sometimes another person expresses exactly what you have just been thinking yourself. Or you observe someone on the street and this person turns around after a certain time, because he or she senses that they are being observed.

I myself felt these deep energetic ties strongly when my father died. I felt it before my mother could tell me. I was a student and had just moved to a new city and had no phone. I knew that my father was in a nursing home because he had Alzheimer's disease. There was no reason to assume that currently something bad could have happened to him, but suddenly I had this strong feeling that he was no longer alive and called his nursing home. I was told that he had been sent to hospital with pneumonia the night before and that he had died in the morning.

I will never forget that feeling that put me in an absolute state of shock. This was the first time in my life that I felt completely lost and experienced how it felt when the ground is lost from under your feet. My mother had sent me a telegram which had not yet reached me. However, I knew the details already. On an energetic level, there was no separation between us. I'll never forget the clock my father had made himself a long time ago. This clock had been hanging in our home in the living room and had worked well for 25 years. The night he died, however, it just stopped working.

Everything is connected to everything

On this deeper level of the energetic quantum field, reality works ·
differently than on the visible, material plane. Things are not ·
bound in time and space and happen not in a linear manner, but ·
they are connected beyond time and space. You may wonder now ·
how can it be that you are connected with the things and people
in your life beyond time and space? In your surroundings everything looks solid and separate from each other. People cannot just
move through everything like a ray of light and "beam" themselves anywhere, as Mr. Spock does in Star Trek.

Of course, we cannot transport ourselves anywhere within
seconds or be in London and Madrid at the same time – as much
as we perhaps would like to sometimes. Amazingly, quanta such
as electrons, however, can do this. This property is related to the
quantum physics concept of "entanglement". Here we encounter ·
another amazing feature of this „other world" on which our
reality is based on. The principle of entanglement says that two
particles that were once joined together as a unit continue to
form a unit even after they have been physically separated from
each other. We can see this because if one part changes, then the
other part spontaneously changes in the same way at the exact
same moment. Albert Einstein called this phenomenon "*spooky
action at a distance.*" Thereby it does not matter whether the two
particles are only one meter, one kilometer or maybe even light
years apart. They remain connected at any distance.

I really started wondering whether you could apply the concept
of entanglement to couples who have been together for a while
when I read about the following. Researchers at the University of
Washington were interested in finding out how strong couples
were linked together energetically. They found out that the energetic entanglement between partners can be so strong that two ·
bodies actually behave as one. They did the following test. They

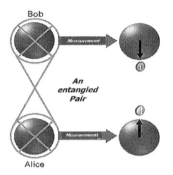

took one partner to a room and asked the other partner to wait in another part of the building. Then they shone a light in the eye of the first partner while studying the ocular and brain reactions of the second partner at the same time. They found that the ocular center of the second partner's brain reacted when the first partner was exposed to the light, even though they were completely separated. In similar experiments the Mexican neuroscientist Jacobo Grinberg-Zylberbaum had already proved the same connection between people who had been meditating together. Classical physics would not be able to explain this, but quantum physics gives us a simple explanation: we are all connected and we are all influencing the world around us through energetic connection.

This was something that Anita Moorjani experienced through her near-death experience and which she portrays vividly. "*I realized that the whole universe is alive and imbued with consciousness and that it includes all of life and the whole of nature. Everything belongs to a boundless whole. In a complex way, I was inextricably linked with all living beings. We are all aspects of this unity - we are all one, and each and every one of us has an effect on the collective whole.*"

Surprisingly enough, these aspects had already been referred to as "Indra's net" in a Mahayana Buddhist sutra. This net demonstrates that everything is not only interconnected with all other things but that everything also reflects the entire network in itself.

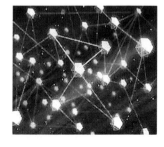

Quantum physics shows us that everything is energetically connected to and entangled with everything. That does not mean, however, that our energy is not individual to us. We each have our own frequency. Our own frequency is how our energy interacts with all the other energies in the field.

Exercise 6

Choose a person that you are having a problem with and start chanting for this person. Whilst chanting, imagine how this person is happy and has all his or her wishes fulfilled. Can you notice a difference?

The field responds to your thoughts and feelings

Best-selling author Gregg Braden teaches us that the energy network that connects everything responds to the instructions of our thoughts and beliefs. For all things in the universe have their own frequency, i.e. their own energy signature and radiating energy, which depends on the particular state of life in which we find ourselves. This also applies to each of our thoughts, feelings and beliefs, which communicate with the quantum network by its own frequency. Therefore, the language of the universe is vibrant energy and through the practice of **daimoku** we learn to communicate with the universe in a dynamic way. By doing so we communicate with the quantum network.

This energetic field acts as a kind of mirror reality: we are part of this field and whatever I experience is what my consciousness reflects back to me. The field responds to my thoughts and feelings by sending me situations and people that are a vibrational match. This in turn means that I first have to change my mind if I want to meet a different "reflection" on the outside.

Doesn't that mean that what you have in your life right now relates to what you've been consciously or unconsciously thinking about in recent days, weeks or months? Well, it certainly means that your life emerges out of your personal vibration. If you are facing negative experiences, you may ask yourself: in what ways do my outer experiences remind me of any negative emotion and thinking I have been involved in recently? You may need to raise your vibration by focusing on things you love and the way you prefer to feel.

The field responds to how we feel and
to what we imagine.

Who do you resonate with?

Energetically speaking, the people in your life are likely a "frequency match" to you. One could say that you attracted them into your life. Their personal vibration is somehow in tune with your own. Your shared vibrations recognize each other's fields. Everything that is in your world "resonates" with you. When people tell you that something resonates with them, they often mean that they feel strongly connected to it on an emotional level. Resonance in quantum physics is very similar. As Braden puts it, *"resonance is an exchange of energy between two things"*. It's a two-way experience allowing something to come into balance with something else. You might also say that two things sync up or tune into each other. Every object or person has a frequency at which it naturally vibrates and if another object or person shares the same energetic frequency they are a frequency match.

Resonating with the frequency of the Gohonzon

When you start chanting **daimoku** to the Gohonzon your own energetic frequency tunes into the frequency of the highest state of consciousness: the enlightened state of life. Once we tune into this highest frequency state, I believe our essential self talks to us. You could put it another way: now you are *in resonance* with your higher self. In that state, we feel it very strongly when our thoughts and emotions, or the people we hang out with, are not in tune with the frequency of our essential self.

I felt this very intensively when I started chanting **daimoku** for the first time. Suddenly I became very sensitive and could not put up with certain people's behavior any more. Additionally, my own negative thoughts and emotions became unbearable to me. At that time, I often pitied myself, thinking I was all alone and had to do everything by myself. Suddenly it occurred to me that this was not true and that there were people out there helping me. I just had to open myself up and contact them. I started resonating with different thoughts and different people.

I realized I had two choices: to feel expanded and connected to the high vibrations of my higher self, or to feel contracted, afraid and immersed in the low vibrations of different kinds of suffering, i.e. to *not* be connected to my higher self. Whenever I choose to feel alone and separate, I start thinking that I have to do every-thing by my own and I start putting myself and the people around me under pressure. Whenever I start chanting, however, I feel connected to something greater than myself and I don't need any pressure or control. Things come to me in a kind of flow and in synchronicity, all at the right time.

An energy field with intelligent consciousness

Everything in this field is immaterial and cannot be perceived by our five senses. Your thoughts are also part of this field. You cannot grab or see your thoughts, but you know that they are there.

As mentioned before, this field connects all things, it is all things, and we are all part of this collective field. This energy field contains all possibilities of the universe as vibrational frequencies. The quantum field is an invisible information field beyond time and space. Dispenza explains that this level is outside of space and time, because the potentials in the quantum field do not yet exist and do not have a location or a position in time. All material forms come from this field and are connected with each other in this field. You and I are connected with each other in this intelligent field that gives life, energy and awareness to all things.

A famous quantum physicist, however, claimed that it's not just energy and information, but in itself a higher intelligence by which this energy is carried and shaped. It was Max Planck who considered this higher intelligence to be the form-giving power behind all appearances. At this time, he already referred to the aspect of a "cosmic consciousness" that is behind all visible manifestations. That becomes very clear in his statement:

> *"There is no matter, but only a web of energies*
> *to which form was given by an intelligent spirit.*
> *This spirit is the source of all matter and not the visible,*
> *but perishable matter. There is no matter as such —*
> *mind is the matrix of all matter."* Max Planck

Now, let us illustrate at this point that reality, according to Max Planck, takes place *on three different dimensions*. Deepak Chopra describes these three planes as follows:

1. The visible, material plane of all things that we perceive, learn and experience with our five senses.
2. The quantum and energy level, which exists simultaneously behind this materialized form, where all phenomena of reality exist as energy and information. There it manifests as vibration.
3. The hidden *virtual plane of pure consciousness,* which we could also call the level of pure potential.

Let´s go through this again. Max Planck had the opinion that at its deepest level matter consists of energy and information, which in turn is controlled by an underlying universal consciousness. Does that also mean that we ourselves are multidimensional beings? What we see and recognize with our senses obviously represents only the first material dimension or level of reality. In plain language, the statements made by Max Planck mean that there is a higher consciousness than my own individual conscious- ness that does not only act within me, but at the same time exists within everybody and everything. It is both personal and univer- sal. In the same way, quantum physicist Paul Wigner considered it as proven that such a higher consciousness exists.

> *"Quantum theory proves the existence of a universal consciousness in the universe."* Paul Wigner

Interestingly enough, these three levels may partially corre- spond to the early Buddhist cosmology which says that the world we live in is subject to Samsara, the cycle of rebirths, and the whole universe consists of three realms where life manifests itself in different ways. These realms are:
1. the realm of desires and sufferings,
2. the realm of form which is free from suffering, and
3. the realm of formlessness.

The last one means a non-material and timeless sphere beyond any perception and can be divided into several spiritual states of mind. These are characterized, for example, as the *sphere of nothingness* or also as the *sphere of infinite consciousness*. These states can also be reached by deep meditation and correspond to the pure consciousness of the universe. In the Nichiren Buddhist tradition this deepest state of mind is called the ninth conscious-ness, which is equivalent to one´s Buddha nature.

The palace of the ninth consciousness

But why should we connect to such a deep state of consciousness? Well, like everything in the universe, we too are connected to a "sea of information" that exists beyond space and time. At this point, it already becomes clear that it is necessary to obtain access to this level in order to be able to choose new opportunities.

> Only at the level of higher consciousness do we really have the opportunity to choose new options.

This level eventually represents the area of pure consciousness, which is also embodied in our individual life as the deepest state of consciousness, which Nichiren described as the "palace of the ninth consciousness". This "ninth consciousness" may be called our higher self and is in connection with the pure, cosmic con-sciousness of the universe. You might call it an individualized form of cosmic consciousness that can act as such within us.

> The cosmic consciousness is embodied in each of us by the "higher self", which is greater and deeper than our everyday ego. In Nichiren Buddhism this is referred to as the deepest level of consciousness, the "ninth consciousness."

When we talk about "cosmic consciousness" we refer to the dimension beyond time and space, as it is described in the "Ceremony in the Air" of the Lotus Sutra. This cosmic consciousness can be both found outside of you as well as inside of you.

Some spiritually minded scientists refer to the quantum field as cosmic consciousness. Dispenza refers to the quantum field as a "*universal intelligence*" or "*universal consciousness*" that animates every aspect of the material universe. When we feel resonance with this loving intelligence, as he also calls it, then we are becoming creators. The important thing is that we are talking about two aspects of consciousness here: The objective consciousness or intelligence of the quantum field, and the subjective consciousness of a free-willed individual.

When our individual consciousness merges with the objective, universal consciousness, that´s when enlightenment takes place. Then this universal intelligence will orchestrate an event or an energetic response to match whatever the subjective mind puts out into the quantum field. That´s why it is so important to clean your emotions and thoughts while chanting – because when you send out the signal of joy, then this universal consciousness will respond by sending into your life joyful events. When you express the feeling of joy, your energy skyrockets. Living in the vibration of joy you attract abundance and all the things that you want in your life. Feeling joy improves all aspects of your life, including your relationships.

Do You feel joyful? Do you feel joy on a daily basis?

Cosmic consciousness as the greatest power

Just when we focus on changing things, it is crucial to recognize that there is something like a "consciousness with a higher intel-

ligence," which is much bigger and more powerful than our everyday consciousness. It is the pure, cosmic consciousness, free of all
negative imprints which represents the same universal force that
makes our heart beat and that creates all the galaxies at the same
time.

It is precisely this universal intelligence that keeps us alive at this
moment. It allows you to pump seven liters of blood through your
body over 100,000 times a day and it makes your body produce
50 million cells in one second. Are you doing all of this consciously
and do you have this whole process under control? Or is it that
these operations are set in motion by an intelligent consciousness
which is much greater than your own individual ego consciousness?

This cosmic consciousness is often described as pure love, for it
is the power that has brought us to life and that keeps us alive.
This intelligent awareness loves you so much that it has called you
into life. The power of this universal consciousness animates
everything physical in this universe. It gives rise to galaxies, makes
your heart beat, while at the same time it ensures that the sea
rises and falls with the tide.

This awareness consists of loving energy that furthermore stops
us from always looking for love and recognition on the outside,
because if we have access to our highest self, which is connected
to cosmic consciousness, we experience the deepest essence of
pure love. In the same way, Anita Moorjani recognized during her
near-death experience that the essence of the entire universe is
pure love: "In my near-death state I realized that the entire universe consists of unconditional love and that I am an expression of
this. (...) In fact, this universal life-force energy is love and I consist
of universal energy!" Thus, to remain faithful to your own higher
self, therefore also includes the extremely important aspect of
self-love and self-respect which is often not taught to us in our
education: "to be love also means that I am aware of how important it is to nourish my own soul, to accept my needs and not

always put myself last." Anita continues to report about her experience: *"When I woke up to my limitless self, I realized to my surprise that my life could be completely different simply by realizing that I am and always have been love. I did not need to do anything to earn love. To understand this means to work with the energy of life-force, whereas I work against it if I make being kind a role play."*

Chapter 7
The Cosmic Mind-Body Fusion

Let´s go back once again to the metaphor of the Ceremony in the Air. There the *empty space* stood for a dimension beyond time and space. In this dimension everything is connected to everything.

> This dimension represents the interconnectedness of all things and an abundance of possibilities presented as potential.

This also applies to the meaning of *the Treasure Tower* which represents these wonderful and precious opportunities at the spiritual, cosmic level. However, what is the meaning of the fact that the two Buddhas, Shakyamuni and Taho, are sitting side by side in the Treasure Tower? What does this really mean and why is it so important for practicing daimoku?

Nichiren explains the interaction of the two Buddhas as the interaction of two factors that are necessary to achieve the state of enlightenment. He compared this interaction to a state in which one´s own individual consciousness is connected to the boundless, pure cosmic consciousness. Nichiren writes in his letter to Mr. Soya in August 1276 that "immediate enlightenment takes place (...) where reality and wisdom are fused into a harmonious unity." This principle is called "fusion of subjective wisdom with objective reality" (*kyōchi-myōgō*). In this case Shakyamuni stands for the aspect of individual, subjective wisdom, and Taho for the aspect of objective, universal reality. Therefore, the two Buddhas symbolize the enlightened state of life, which will be realized by chanting daimoku. So far this is the standard answer in Nichiren Buddhist study.

I remember quite vividly the first time I heard this explanation. I thought to myself: what the hell does "objective reality" mean? I could figure out what my subjective wisdom could be, but what does it mean when it "fuses with objective reality"? It does sound a little bit abstract, don´t you think?

Energized focus in a state of flow

Therefore we may first apply this principle to the things that we experience in our daily life in order to understand the meaning of it. Imagine that you are engaged in a creative activity like writing a thesis or playing a musical instrument. Whenever you are involved in your activity in such a way that you forget yourself, time and even your environment, you experience a harmonious unity with the object that you are working with. This is nothing but the mental state of "flow" in which you are completely absorbed in what you are doing. You are fully immersed in a feeling of energized focus and enjoyment. This mental state of immersion and concentration has something to do with the meaning of "ichinen". Do you remember? That´s when you are completely tuned into this present moment! In this state of flow, you may notice that it´s not your everyday self, but something greater than you, like your higher self, that is active in the process.

Let´s go one step further and transfer this experience you may have in daily life to the level of cosmic consciousness. The universe as the objective reality has no boundary and is therefore unlimited. When you fuse into a harmonious unity with this cosmic consciousness, your individual consciousness will also become unlimited. Then you are in the state of enlightenment. That is when you are pure consciousness. In this state of life your subjective wisdom is capable of "enlightening and unfolding this essence of all phenomena". In this state you are able to understand the meaning of life and all the experiences that you have, you are free from all sufferings, and you are able to unfold your entire capacities and possibilities.

The merging of your individual consciousness with cosmic consciousness is symbolically expressed by the two Buddhas, Shakyamuni and Taho in the Treasure Tower. This principle is called *kyōchi-myōgō*.

Feel the energy of kyōchi-myōgō

Now we can apply the principle of kyōchi-myōgō to our daily practice to the Gohonzon. Since the daimoku contains the "unlimited wisdom" of higher self in connection with cosmic consciousness, this fusion happens when we recite daimoku intensively to the mandala inscribed by Nichiren. When, by doing so, we entirely merge with the Gohonson, the object for meditative focus, and only perceive this Gohonson whilst forgetting our environment, our body and time at the same moment: That's when our own individual consciousness connects with the cosmic consciousness. Only then are we in kyōchi-myōgō.

This meditative state of being completely one with the Gohonzon is often experienced during daimoku chanting, when a strong flow of energy and joy rises from the bottom to the top of one's body. In this case one often feels a very clear feeling at the top or the front side of one's head. At the same time one can feel a vitalizing, soothing and cleansing energy throughout one's whole body.

When you are being one with the Gohonzon,
that's when you are a Buddha!

Exercise 7

Whenever you reach the state of being one with the Gohonzon, what exactly do you feel? What happens in your mind and your body?

Getting beyond yourself

Many of our practitioners often ask us whether they should free themselves from any thoughts and wishes, or whether they should set a goal and concentrate on it during daimoku chanting. In any case it doesn't make sense to remain in the state of your daily consciousness of the small and restless ego. Thus it is better to first enter into the meditative state of your higher self in connection with the cosmic consciousness. If then, during the chanting of daimoku, we dissolve in such a way that we forget ourselves, our previous identities and time, then we are in kyōchi-myōgō.

When, whilst chanting, you get to a place where you are *no-body*, *no-thing*, no-where and no-time, that's the moment that you are literally pure consciousness. That's when your subjective mind has fused with cosmic consciousness. It is the energy of cosmic consciousness that changes your life. It is only pure consciousness that changes your ego. Your ego can never change your ego. When you reach this state, where you disconnect from your body and forget about your life, then you can change your life. Once you forget about who you are, when you forget that you are a woman or a man, a father, a mother, a wife, a husband, a lawyer, a teacher, a bank clerk, a vegetarian, a Buddhist or a certain nationality – when you get beyond all the elements that you identify with, that's the moment that you can begin to change your life.

We have seen so many changes happening that we can say: We are at our absolute best when we get beyond ourselves. Once we are in this state, we can then identify and clarify what we want and concentrate on it during the practice of daimoku to the Gohonzon. Now we have access to the field of all possibilities.

The Gohonzon: the sea of all possibilities

I had realized why Nichiren had inscribed the Mandala: it provides access to this enlightened dimension. He made it available to us so that we can enter this holy, mystical world full of potential. This happens when we completely trust the mandala: "*All of my, Nichiren's, disciples and believers should enter the Treasure Tower of this Gohonzon, because they sincerely believe in it*" (»Reply to Nichinyo« of 1278).

When we recite the dharma as a mantra in front of the mandala, then we take part in the Ceremony in the Air, that is, this sacred event in a mythical past that is happening at the present moment. When we step out of the everyday time dimension we have direct access to a timeless dimension. There is no past and no future. Everything happens simultaneously.

Only here do we find access to all the possibilities of the Treasure Tower that are waiting for us. These are not in our outer life, but unfold only when we experience them in connection with cosmic consciousness. This is what Nichiren´s words indicate: *"Never seek this Gohonzon outside yourself. It only exists within the flesh of your chest where you embrace the Lotus Sutra and chant Nam-myōhō-renge-kyō. This is called the palace of the absolute truth of mind in the ninth consciousness"* (»Answer to Ms. Nichinyo (The Real Aspect of the Gohonzon)« of 1278).

The Gohonzon can be simply regarded as the energetic signature of enlightened consciousness. When you sit in front of the mandala, you see in it your own enlightened consciousness. For Nichiren´s mandala acts like a mirror of a special kind, which always reflects your enlightened life. By chanting you align your individual consciousness to the cosmic consciousness.

Once again it was Anita Moorjani who made it clear to me that at the level of cosmic consciousness there exists no time. I started to realize that this level really exists, because she had experienced it through her near-death experience: *"Even time felt differently in this realm and I felt every moment simultaneously. I was aware of everything that concerned me at the same time – past, presence and future. I became aware of lives that seemed to happen simultaneously. In one incarnation I seemed to have a younger brother."*

Nichiren´s mandala provides a direct access to this mythical event in "sacred time". There is only the present. When during chanting we forget everything around us, we have access to that level where anything is possible.

Myō, or, to be fully equipped

One of the meanings of the syllable "Myō" is "to be fully equipped." This means that *myō*, which also means "the mystical, wonderful and hidden", represents the spiritual level of potential in terms of the abundance of possibilities. In relation to our life, it means that we all have the skills and potential to be completely happy. Our individual life, as it is, is not characterized by lack but has in itself all the possibilities for the concrete fulfillment of all possibilities.

The principle "Myō-Hō" (the Mystic Law) shows us that on the outside we are confronted with what we created ourselves – mostly unconsciously, and sometimes even against our own will. In any case, it shows where we put our focus on. If we take into consideration that the outer, material reality only represents the manifestation of a tiny portion of 0.00001% (of the total potential), then there are 99.99999% other options available to us that we can choose.

So why do we always focus so vehemently
on this materialized form of reality,
while 99.99999% of reality is available to us?

If then we "observe" the state which we focus on over and over again with concentration and attention, then this desired state will unfold in our life. By practicing daimoku in front of the Gohonzon we consciously observe a reality chosen by us, thus changing our existing reality.

Since Myō also has the meaning "to be completely equipped", Myō also represents the level of the non-visible, the level of potential. According to the quantum spiritual model this level exists beyond time and space at the level of cosmic consciousness. There, everything is not only possible, but it already exists. The same applies to the quantum field at the level of pure potential:

all potential experiences exist there as energetic frequency patterns in the "sea of infinite potential".

You may imagine it this way: energetically speaking everything already exists, i.e. there is an energy signature for success, happiness, prosperity, health and for love. All these things already exist as an energetic frequency pattern. Every human being and all matter is constantly emitting a certain energy pattern that contains information. If you could change your energy signature in a way as to match an already existing signature in the field, then the probability is high to be attracted by this event.

The event will "find" you in your new reality. Any possibility, like for instance a new house, a new job or a new partner, already exists as a vibrational frequency. When we align our own frequency pattern with this potential, then we come into resonance with it. The potential templates of this new reality go into resonance with the energetic radiance of people, similar to the tuning fork effect: Like attracts like.

> We must first energetically become
> what we intent to achieve.

On the level of pure potential all these possibilities exist as energetic frequency patterns. This level is represented by the

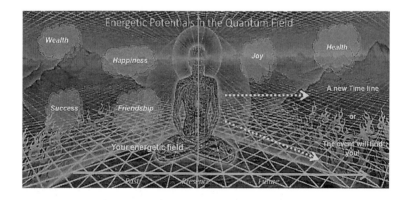

Treasure Tower in the Lotus Sutra. But how do we align ourselves
to this existing potential on this level? How do we become,
energetically, what we intend to be?

Fulfill your wishes by transforming your energy

A Turkish participant of our seminars who had already been
practicing with us for four years told us about an interesting
experience of hers that illustrates beautifully what it means to
energetically become what you intend to be. She was already 40
years old and had been working as a hairdresser for the past
twenty years. She was the mother of a small child and at the time
she was stuck in a rather frustrating and energy-consuming relationship. Due to her own migrant background she knew what it
meant to get established in a foreign culture as a single woman.
She started to practice daimoku and firmly decided to change her
professional and private situation. She wanted to study and start
a completely new profession in the social field. At the beginning,
her environment did not take her quite seriously. But every day,
when she took her son to kindergarten, she walked past the
university where she had applied to become a student.

> In her mind she already saw herself studying there
> and entering this building every day.

She told her little son that she would soon be studying there.
She chanted in a very focused manner with the clear objective to
be accepted as a student and to get financial support for her
studies. Her chances were not promising. There were a lot of
applicants, and only a few of them would get a place at the
university. Yet, inside she already felt like she was studying.

One day she called me and proudly announced that daimoku had
worked. As a matter of fact, only 120 out of 1,500 applicants had
been accepted by the university. And she was one of them. Today

she is about to finish her studies. She also completely transformed her private situation. At the beginning, her partner even threatened to kill her if she should leave him. In the end everything turned out fine and he who moved out peacefully, and she could find a new apartment for her and her son. This had also been an image she had held with clarity, and she had already emotionally felt it whilst chanting.

When we already feel and experience
what we want to achieve whilst chanting,
then we energetically become what we want to be.

We can observe this in our daily life. Have you ever had the experience that when you are unhappy, more and more aspects occur in your life that confirm and reinforce this dissatisfaction? The train is late that is supposed to take us to an urgent appointment and the food at our favorite Italian restaurant is salty or our employees are in an extremely bad mood. In any case we encounter many inconveniences that further evoke the feeling of dissatisfaction. If, in contrast, we send out the feeling of appreciation and gratitude, then we experience things that reinforce this feeling of appreciation within us.

On the other hand, you may have the experience that often unexpected opportunities arise when, through practicing **daimoku,** you are resonating with your unlimited state of consciousness. Then we "coincidentally" meet someone who can allow us a career boost or we realize that today the people in the supermarket are very nice at the checkout. This in turn means that:

The field reacts to the energetic signature
of our thoughts and feelings.

All material and every person radiates a certain energy pattern, a certain energetic signature that contains information about this person´s feelings and thoughts, i.e. this person´s state of life. It is our own energetic signature that determines with which option in the sea of all possibilities we resonate, for there are an infinite number of options.

According to the mechanistic and materialistic worldview, according to which everything is happening outside of ourselves, we are first waiting to become rich on the outside, before we feel rich and happy. The quantum spiritual model, however, tells us the contrary: we must first feel inwardly rich and happy and radiate joy, and then we attract the corresponding circumstances on the outside.

Why are we not sending out signals that match what we want to achieve?

Of course, this is not easy when the corresponding "reality" looks very different and we have to deal with unemployment, illness, dysfunctional relationships or legal disputes on the outside. But here the power of daimoku is revealed, because with the Gohonzon Nichiren has given us a means to access the level of pure consciousness and to observe the desired reality before the mandala.

We can purify our negative emotions with the effect of being perfectly happy "for no reason" after an intensive practice of daimoku. When we manage to keep this positive emotional state together with a clear intention (to be healthy or to make professional or financial progress) again and again, then we soon notice the first signs and support that are in our external reality. We are in resonance with a new reality and "by coincidence" new opportunities arise and new doors open through which we are challenged to go. These findings shatter our idea that we are separate from our environment and that things just happen around us, and that we have no influence.

The quantum spiritual model indicates that our environment is an extension of our own consciousness. In Nichiren Buddhism this principle is called *eshō-funi*. Very often we think that we have no choice and we are desperate. But we live in a world of endless options, of which we have just chosen a small fraction up to now.

We may therefore consider our own personal situation, condition and external reality of our life as only one possible reality.

Imagine that countless versions of our current situation were played simultaneously in several theaters at the same time. We only need one ticket to another performance, but this ticket is not valid for a performance on the level of our rational mind. It does, however, give us access to the level beyond time and space. In the Lotus Sutra, this level is portrayed metaphorically as the *Ceremony in the Air* and the ticket enables us to take part in this ceremony, as well as it gives us access to the Treasure Tower that contains all options.

Now at this moment, we are in one of these theatres, watching one particular performance, but by changing our energetic frequency through the practice of daimoku we do have the opportunity to see one of the alternate shows – i.e. manifest a different option in our life. This is exactly what Anita Moorjani experienced during her near-death experience. She experienced a state of consciousness in which she realized that life is like a large warehouse in which there are infinite possibilities from which we can choose.

However, the focus of our consciousness is usually so narrow that it seems as if we had only a small flashlight in order to illuminate familiar options and to choose them again and again. However, we only experience the things to which we have directed our focus. In the state of pure consciousness, Anita saw this warehouse all of a sudden as if "lit by a floodlight" and now recognized the infinite variety of other options that she simply had not perceived previously. *"It´s there, but your light is not directed to it (...) You realize that what you previously thought was your reality, is really little more than a spark of that immeasurable miracle that surrounds you. (...) You notice innumerous things in this warehouse you have never seen before, whose existence in this splendor of colors, tones and texture you have not even dreamt of."*

> In the state of pure consciousness we are in a room full of possibilities: you select what you put your focus on.

Transforming poison into medicine

Of course, it is not easy to make yourself "independent" from your external situation, when everything collapses on the outside. However, it is possible to do so with **daimoku**.

To give a personal example, my husband and I never thought that our plan to build a house would develop into such a dramatic challenge in our Buddhist practice. The whole process has not only shown us that in this case our "individual karma" was constantly at work, but that this process was also embedded at a cultural level and was accompanied by country-specific karma. With "karma" we mean the way to think, to feel and to behave. At the individual level the force of our own karma hit us in terms of uncertainty and fear that were connected with this project, when the company Yukio worked for was sold to a foreign investor and his position removed. This meant that shortly before we started building the house he had lost his supposedly safe and very well-paid job.

This blow could have not come at a worse time, and of course caused extreme fear and uncertainty about whether we should start to build the house considering this situation. However, to build this house had also been one of our visions we wanted to realize because we wanted to use it as our **daimoku** practicing center and research institute. We relied on the power of **daimoku** and to be able to transform this situation and not let the external conditions distract us from our construction project. In addition, we realized that the external situation also reflected our own fears and so we had to have clear determination to overcome them, if we really wanted to build the house. Whilst chanting we focused our thoughts on the image that the house was already built and that we had sufficient funds available. Every time we were in a state of deep focus we felt that, at the level of cosmic consciousness, there is no shortage and that we were really fully equipped.

As it turned out later, it was a real "blessing" that Yukio had lost his job at that moment. Whilst we were building the house there were so many technical issues the construction company let us completely down with. I could have not solved these problems without Yukio's presence and without his technical knowledge.

We learned that in Germany you can never fully trust any construction company and that you always have to control any construction work. Moreover, Yukio was still fully paid by his old company for a whole year, although the new owner of the company had exempted him from work. Furthermore, we achieved such a large settlement in court that even our lawyer was amazed at the amount of the sum. Before this hearing we focused all our thoughts on a large settlement payment when chanting to the Gohonzon. We needed this payment in order to continue to build the house.

When the house was finally built and "only" in-house work needed to be done, Yukio again got a lucrative job that he gratefully accepted. The interesting point here was that we could easily have done without all the anxiety and the fear beforehand, because all this time we were "protected". Only later did we realize that we could have never handled all this stress whilst also being fully employed. But the best thing was: a new well-paid job and new source of income came again at the "right time", when the hardest and toughest construction phase was over. It was really mystical.

The "external benefits" came always as a clear result of our changes in our own consciousness and in our attitude. The more we overcame our fears and worries and the more we felt fully equipped and supplied, the clearer the benefits appeared on the outside. The whole time we felt very strongly that finishing the house was all about the last visible manifestation of our long and sometimes hard and painful process of a big internal development. We had to learn to stand up against cunning building companies and to fully commit ourselves to our building project in order to really stand our ground. At the end, however, it became almost natural for us to do so.

> Master yourself and at the end of this self-conquering there is the reality that you have been focusing on all the time.

As our financial situation had developed so positively, the following year we built another house in Japan. We experienced a big difference between building a house in Germany and in Japan. In Japan the house was built within three months and we could leave all the work to the respective craftsmen, without having to check on them. This was when we realized that it had not only been our individual karma, but also a great portion of the respective country's karma we had to confront.

> Focus clearly on what you want and not on what you don´t want.

We should send out positive energies

Energetically we are always confronted with what we "send out". Therefore, it is absolutely necessary to transform one's own negative emotions if we want to create a happier reality on the outside. However, it is not enough just to change one's thoughts and to think "positive" from now on. As we shall see, it is absolutely necessary to align both our thoughts *and* our feelings to achieve one new overall condition. This creates a very specific state of life that contains an energy signature that influences each atom in our life. It is therefore very important to change our life condition in order to attract new experiences into our lives.

The changes of your inner world cause
the changes of your outer world.

Once we have really come to understand this, we should ask ourselves what thoughts and feelings we unconsciously send out every day. Thoughts and emotions are energy. The energy that we put out, however, is the same energy that we attract back to our lives. If you want to draw positive people, things and situations into your life, then you have to elevate your own energetic state in order to emit a higher vibrational energy. You wonder how one can increase one's energy? Our findings have shown that practicing daimoku is an extremely efficient method for doing so.

Your own energy field

The new sciences that are now integrating energy and consciousness keep saying that we are *"energetic, vibrational beings"* living in an "energetic, vibrational universe". In scientific terms, vibration can be translated as energy and this energy has a lot to do with about what we think and how we feel and how we live our lives. The human body is not just the gross physical parts that we feel, see or smell. Our body also has a subtle body that you cannot see. Everyone is surrounded by an energy field that changes according to their own state of consciousness. Our words, emotions and thoughts create a vibratory field. When the field becomes strong enough, it can attract similar vibrations. This has been known for quite a long time, but we now live in a technologically advanced age where it is possible to measure the energetic structures in our body.

Modern energy medicine says that the energy field of a human being stores all psychological and physical experiences. It stores positive experiences and negative experiences. Negative experiences, however, will often manifest as blockages in your body and hinder the energy flow. This often leads to physical or emotional pain. In my experience, the energy of daimoku is able to clean and transform these blockages. Then your energy can flow freely again. I have experienced this many times. Now we were trying to find out whether it was possible to measure these energetic changes.

Chapter 8
The Measurable Effects of DaimokuPower

Electrophtonical Measurment

We were fascinated by the idea that it might be possible to measure our own energy fields. Was there a way to make our own energy emissions visible? We investigated and came across a method that in the meantime had become very common in Russia and in the US in various areas of medicine and consciousness research, and which is successfully used by several Olympic teams. This is the measurement technology of electrophotonics, or GDV (Gas Discharge Visualization). This gas discharge technology gives great insight into the nature of your own personal energy state.

Electrophotonics is a modern variation of energy field measurement that was developed in 1996 by the Russian professor of physics, Dr. Konstantin Korotkov. Through this method it is possible to map the energy field of a human body.

This method of bio-electrography actually goes back to the German physicist Georg Lichtenberg (1742-1799). He realized that his finger shone with a bright, blue light when he put it on a glass plate that covered an electrode under high voltage. Science calls this phenomenon "coronal discharge", where plasma, or ions, absorb energy in the field and stimulate the gas atoms to glow.

In the 1930s a Russian couple called Kirlian developed a world-famous form of radiographic imagery ("Kirlian photography"). They had found a way to record the coronal discharge of objects on photographic paper or plates.

The researchers noted an inexplicable link between the glowing in the pictures and the condition of the objects. They wondered if

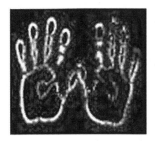  

Kirlian's photography

there was some information encoded in the scanned coronal discharge. Since the mid-1980s Dr. Konstantin Korotkov has made this question the central area of his research. For this purpose he developed the GDV technique in 1996, which employed the use of digital recording technology and modern computers to record the emission of living objects in what is now known as the "Kirlian method". This digital method means that the measurement is always available and comparable. This helped Prof. Korotkov to further develop within this field, which is commonly referred to as "electrophotonics". Kirlian photography is now an easy-to-use diagnostic technology with which the human energy field can be represented in real time. It is believed that Kirlian photography enables for physical, emotional, mental and even spiritual states to be converted into graphic images.

We send light in the form of photons and electrons

By using a digital GDV camera Korotkov managed to record and portray the energy that is put out by each of us. This energy field can be measured at the individual fingertips which are assigned to the individual organs of the human body with reference to tradi-tional Chinese medicine (TCM). Those are the same twelve meridi-ans that also play an important role in acupuncture.

With a simple finger scan, an electromagnetic field is generated on a glass plate. This causes a weak, visible discharge of photons and electrons which become visible in a glowing of the fingertips. This energy is recorded by sensitive digital cameras and transmitted to a computer. With the help of special software programs, the energy reserves, the quality of the energy and the energy distribution in a human body are determined. At the end the entire energy field of a person can be imaged. This energy field is a subtle extension of one's physical body. These recordings give valuable information about your own state of health and about your momentary stress level.

The GDV measurement is also used to determine the effect of certain substances or mental influences on the energy field of a person. We found this very interesting and we wanted to test whether the practice of daimoku had an effect on one's energy field. Would the chanting of daimoku cause energetic changes? Was there a noticeable difference in one's own energy field after ten minutes of daimoku? Was there a way to measure the effect of daimoku?

Daimoku changes your energy field

Since we are energetic beings and Nichiren's Gohonzon contains the energy signature of the highest life state, ten minutes of intense daimoku should be enough to cause a change in one's energetic vibrational field. We had experienced that many times before. Every time, I was amazed at how much a negative emotional state like anger, sadness or fear could be transformed in a very short time by deep focused practice. Every time, a deep feeling of happiness rises up inside and suddenly you feel energy, confidence and a positive outlook again. We wanted to know, however, if this psychosomatic change caused by chanting daimoku was measurable and what it actually looked like.

Our energy measurement appointment took us a long way by train. Even the day before we were up very early and travelled all day. Late at night we arrived at our destination. Then it took us another three quarters of an hour to take the subway to our hotel. We went to bed completely exhausted. The next morning, we got up early to take part in a training session on GDV measurement.

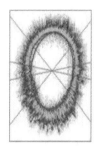

Finger scan with the GDV-Camera

At our appointment, we had our current statuses measured. I knew I was pretty exhausted. Hence, the result of the first measurement revealed a few particular weaknesses. I could see them in the picture as individual holes in my energy field. The analysis stunned us. The expert pointed to physical vulnerabilities in detail that we had known for a long time. For more than twenty years I have had hypothyroidism, which has been treated with thyroid hormones. For a few months my doctor had been steadily reducing the dosage. Since then I did not feel fit and well. However, I had already forgotten that I was taking less thyroid hormones and did not think that this could be the reason for my physical condition. The measuring of my energy field and the subsequent detailed analysis of the result showed that I had a current energetic deficit in the area of the thyroid. We were very surprised that all the other details were completely true as well. Any known physical vulnerability was found in an energy shortage in the appropriate place.

After this first measurement we chanted daimoku intensively for ten minutes before the Compact-Gohonzon that we had taken with us. It had an energizing effect as usual, and immediately I felt much better. I felt much more energy than before. Immediately after the daimoku our fingertips were scanned and our energy fields were measured. Had the perceived energetic changes become visible? Was it really possible to measure the altered state of mine which was caused by the ten minutes of daimoku?

We did not have to wait long for the result. We could clearly see it on my second energy scan now: the measurement result showed that the previous gaps or blockages had largely disappeared and were filled up with energy again. At the points that had previously shown weaknesses, a closed and clear energy field could be seen again. The entire energy picture looked much stronger after daimoku and formed a closed and refilled energy shield. Only ten minutes of intense daimoku to Mandala-Gohonzon had been enough to replenish my energy reserves. I did not just feel it, but my energy scan showed it clearly. Furthermore, my "stress factor" had been reduced from 3.5 to 2.6. And all this in just ten minutes.

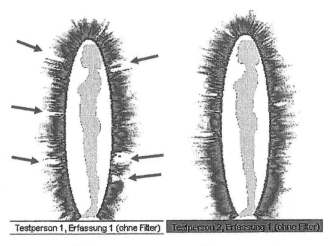

Testperson 1, Erfassung 1 (ohne Filter)   Testperson 2, Erfassung 1 (ohne Filter)

Before daimoku   *After daimoku*

We knew that we wanted to do more research in this direction and that in the future we would make many more measurements on the participants of our seminar to get even more comparisons. For the time being, however, this visible proof of the effect of daimoku was enough for us.

> By practicing daimoku to the Gohonzon
> we raise our own vibrational energy which then acts
> as a shield against external attacks.

The scientist who developed the energy field measurement, Dr. Konstantin Korotkov, repeatedly reports on the positive influence that meditation has on a person's energy field. He says that this is because meditation leads to a positive resonance with the universal quantum field and thus activates innumerable positive potentials on the physical, psychological and energetic level. These positive energetic changes, which are activated by a positive resonance to the quantum field, show themselves again in one's individual energy field and can then be measured by the GDV technology. Practicing daimoku obviously represents such a resonant bridge to the universal quantum field and leads to a positive resonance with it.

> The practice of daimoku, a mantra meditation, creates
> a positive resonance to the universal quantum field
> and enhances our individual energy field.

Chapter 9
The Energetic Frequency of the Chakras

The seven energy centers in your body

Besides your own energy field that your body radiates and which surrounds your body like a shell, there is another factor that plays a major role in describing the energetic state of a person: his or her energy centers, described in Hindu or Buddhist literature as "chakras".

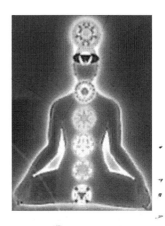

They are described as rotating wheels or colored lotus leaves that rotate at different speeds as they process energy. Each body is enlivened by these seven energy centers that run from the lower pelvic floor along the spine up to the head, and which determine your own physical and emotional states; they control the flow of the vital life energy that fills the physical body with vitality and that keeps it alive.

Only recently have the energy centers also been acknowledged by some Western medicine. A lot of research into the effects of acupuncture on the energy meridians and other Oriental healing methods have drawn attention on the energy centers. In recent decades there were even interesting studies about individual researchers who developed special instruments to measure the energy field that surrounds the individual energy centers. Thus, in energy medicine it is generally accepted that health disorders show up early in the energy field of a person and in their energy centers long before they manifest on the physical level.

The energy centers are a kind of interconnected power system. Thus, the nature of your own energy field depends on the activity of the individual energy centers, because it is animated by the energy flow that occurs in the rotating chakras. Everything in our universe radiates energy. Even our cells give off energy. Thus the chakras are seen as channels that are located at the corners of the body through which energy can constantly flow in and out. The chakra's energy is supposed to rotate clockwise when moving your body's energy out into the external energy field, and it rotates counter-clockwise when it draws energy externally into your body.

That means that your energy field is in constant motion, transporting energy in and out of your physical body. At the same time our energy field also acts as the memory of our own thought forms and emotions. Therefore, the energy centers also represent the connection between our body and our consciousness. Everything in our life can thus be influenced when we activate this energy system. On the physical level, however, the individual energy centers are assigned to a particular area of the organs.

How are the energy centers related to consciousness?

Your consciousness, that is, the way how you perceive your reality, stands for all the possibilities that you can experience. Therefore, when you feel tension in one specific area of your consciousness, then you also feel the tension in the chakra that is associated with that part of your consciousness. Consequently, you are also likely to experience this tension in the body parts that are associated with this chakra.

This in turn means that the physical location at which you experience this tension and stress may serve as an indication as to why you are tense and stressed out. If, for example, you feel hurt in a relationship, then you might feel this tension in your heart. If you are nervous or anxious, it will show in a weak bladder. If you feel tension in a certain part of your consciousness and therefore in the chakra that is connected to this part of your consciousness, then this tension is taken up by the nerve plexus that is associated with this chakra and communicated to the body parts that is controlled by this nerve plexus.

If this tension continues for a prolonged time or reaches a certain degree of intensity, then this creates a lasting symptom on the physical level. In this case the symptom tells us through our body what has previously taken place in our consciousness.

The opening and closing of the chakras

The opening and closing of the chakras works like an energetic defense system. A negative experience and negative emotions that have a low frequency can cause the respective chakra to close, in order to block this energy. If we cling to a feeling of a low frequency, such as guilt, sadness or anxiety and amplify these emotions, because we refuse to confront them or to move them energetically, then the corresponding chakra closes. Thereby the channel is blocked. Each of the emotions that is located at the lower end of the life conditions can trigger a narrowing of the chakras. The corresponding emotions are then stored in our body. We often feel this narrowing of the chakras as a tension in our body when we are stressed. However, when we chant daimoku intensively, this leads to an opening and activating of the chakras. This way we can release the previously stored and jammed energy of the negative emotions and the energy jam is dissolved.

Daimoku dissolves energetic blockages.

I often observed this in myself when suddenly, during intensive chanting, tears started welling up and blocked emotions were released. This is a good sign that there has begun the dissolution of the energetic blockage that held your own consciousness in a low frequency.

Exercise 8

* When you feel that you are in a restricted energetic condition, take a few minutes during the day to focus and chant.

  If you are not at home, focus inwardly on the image of your Gohonzon and on the sound of **daimoku**.

  If possible, recite the mantra **Nam-myō-hō-ren-ge-kyō** aloud.

* At the sound of **daimoku**, stop trying to control the situation and allow the vibration of the mantra to clean the internal chatter of your head.

- -

Measurable changes in the energy centers

During the preliminary GDV measurement of our energy field, my husband and I found that further conclusions could be drawn from the same data that – apart from the above mentioned changes in the energy field of your body – indicated the changes in our individual energy centers. This way it was possible to calculate the amount of energy and the physiological and emotional balance of all chakras. Of course I wanted to know more about this, and was excited to see what changes ten minutes of **daimoku** would cause in my energy centers. First, a baseline measurement of my energy centers was performed. The result was as follows:

Despite the fact that on the day of the measurement I had the feeling that I felt stressed and exhausted, the arrangement of the energy centers appeared surprisingly "straight", i.e. largely harmonious and centered from top to bottom. The owners of the institute who had taken the measurement said that this indicated that I had been "meditating" for quite a while. Many years of practicing **daimoku** had aligned my energy centers in the center and they were almost exactly at the place where they were supposed to be.

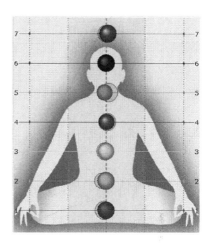

However, this is not always the case and can therefore not be automatically expected. The individual energy centers can be very much out of balance due to stress and emotional strain, as shown in the results of another participant who was simultaneously measured that day under the same conditions. This third person had never practiced meditation before. The recording shows that the energy of this person was very disrupted and that the energy centers of this person were very small, i.e. that very low energy activity was exhibited. At the same time the energy centers were also not aligned at all, which indicated that the emotional and energetic balance of this participant was currently upset. However, he was so friendly and allowed us to use the result of the measurement of his current energetic state.

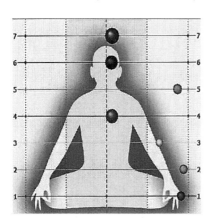

A person without any meditation experience

Activating the energy centers through daimoku

After the initial measurement we chanted ten minutes of intensive **daimoku** to the portable Gohonzon we had brought. Of course,
we were very interested to see whether our **daimoku** session of ten
minutes had caused a visible and measureable change in the
activity of our energy centers. Would the measurement show a
change? The result was as follows:

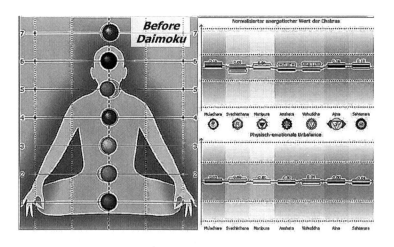

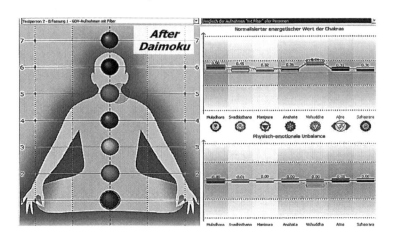

The individual energy centers were now even more precisely positioned, although they had been almost exactly positioned at where they were supposed to be right from the outset. What was striking, however, was the increased activity in the individual energy centers, which had visibly become bigger. This occurred mainly in the first energy center, which appears as red, and the fifth energy center, which appears as light blue. The graphical representation of the enlarged energy centers therefore corresponds to the concrete values, which had also risen accordingly.

Energy Center		Energetical Value	
	Color	Before daimoku	After daimoku
Seventh energy center	Lilac	0.18	0.30
Sixth energy center	Dark blue	0.16	0.31
Fifth energy center	Light blue	-0.11	0.74
Fourth energy center	Green	-0.10	0.36
Third energy center	Yellow	0.04	0.32
Second energy center	Orange	0.09	0.45
First energy center	Red	0.16	0.50

The result of my initial measurement showed that the energetic values of my energy centers were within the normal range that day. Thus, in the initial measurement the first energy center of the color red (first energy center at the bottom), for example, showed an energetic value of 0.16 before daimoku activation. After ten minutes of daimoku, however, this value had changed drastically and had risen to 0.50.

> In the first energy center alone, the readings had
> increased by a little more than three times
> after ten minutes of daimoku.

All other values in the other energy centers had risen similarly. However, the most drastic increase was found in the exact energy center where my energy field had showed an energetic deficiency when measured earlier: in the fifth energy center, which is assigned to the throat and the thyroid area and which shows as a light blue.

It was striking that through daimoku activation it was possible to "refill" such a significant deficiency in such a way that exactly this point showed the largest increase of energy, i.e. the energetic value of the energy center. The energetic value had increased from −0.11 to +0.74 in only ten minutes. This means that the energetic value of this energy center or chakra was increased almost eight-fold by daimoku activation. Activating the chakras through daimoku obviously leads to an energetic balance and to a balancing of the energy centers, which depends on the current frequency of the energy centers.

Thus, the change or activation of the energy centers through the practice of daimoku could be concretely represented and measured. Ten minutes of daimoku had partly caused up to a threefold increase in the activation of the individual energy centers. The biggest energy rise, however, occurred exactly in the energy center which had previously shown the biggest energy deficiency.

> Daimoku has the effect that energetic deficits are being
> replenished in a particularly efficient and powerful way.

Daimoku and the individual energy centers

In many traditions, the energy centers play a major role not only for one's own physical and emotional state, but also for one's own personal and spiritual growth. That is because your own spiritual growth is often equated with the opening and activating of your own energy centers. This in turn means that the quality of life is highly dependent on the opening, cleaning and activating of the individual energy centers.

I had clearly seen via the GDV measurement that the energy in the energy centers had been highly increased through a short daimoku. Therefore, I wondered whether in Nichiren Buddhism itself there was any in-depth reference to the concept of the seven energy centers. If they played such an important role in so many old traditions, then Nichiren must have been aware of this concept. I already knew that Nichiren mentioned the energy centers in his "Orally transmitted teachings" from the year 1280:

> One can also say that our head [*head chakra*] is assigned to the syllable "myō", our throat [*throat chakra*] to the syllable "hō", our chest [*heart chakra*] to the syllable "ren", our stomach [*navel chakra*] to the syllable "ge" and our legs [*root chakra*] to the syllable "kyō".

When we apply this to the seven characters of Na-m(u)-myō-hō-ren-ge-kyō, they also correspond to the seven energy centers, which in general only appear in later Buddhist teachings. However, they had obviously already been known to Nichiren in their basic form. Therefore, I

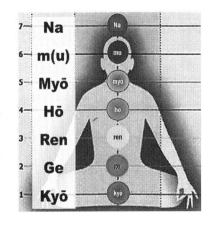

would like to talk about the individual energy centers in more detail, since they perfectly illustrate the effect of **daimoku.**

A feeling of happiness rises from bottom to top

The activation of life force that is a result of the practice of **daimoku** shows itself concretely in an activation of the individual energy centers. This can often be felt clearly in a very concrete way. Many of our participants have reported that even after the first recitation of **daimoku** a strong energetic feeling of happiness rises within them from bottom to top. We ourselves have experienced this countless times.

> During intense **daimoku** practice a strong and clearly palpable energy flow rises from bottom to top.

At the same time, in those moments I always feel great vitality and vigor, and a very strong mental and emotional clarity ascending in me that energizes me enormously.

> The energy rising through the practice of **daimoku** is always accompanied by a great feeling of happiness and a strong feeling of energization and clarity.

How exactly do these energy centers look and which areas of the body and of one´s own personal development are associated with them?

What do the seven energy centers stand for?

According to ancient wisdom, when a meditative expansion of our consciousness occurs, new energy is taken in through the seven subtle energy centers, which represent a connection between our physical body and our spiritual, energetic body. One could say that these centers represent the source of our life energy, whereby the energy flows from the lowest to the highest energy center. Thus, there is a dynamic connection between the lowest and the highest energy center.

Each of these energy centers is directly associated with an organ or a physical or psychological function. That's why each of these centers has a specific task both in the physical as well as in the psychological and energetic areas. Since GDV measurement shows how a disease already shows on an energetic level before it manifests on the physical level, it is relatively easy to find out the energetic cause of physical or emotional disease when you know which areas of the body are related to the seven energy centers.

The first energy center (Kyō): vitality and security

The first energy center is associated with the color red and can be found at the "root" of the body, at the very base of your spine at the perineum area, and is therefore also called the "root chakra". According to the traditional teachings its influence plays a vital role for our life force.

When this chakra is low on energy or is blocked, then you often feel a lot of fear or you might be "overly intellectual". This energy center also has an influence on one's sense of belonging. Therefore, a blockage of this center manifests itself as a feeling of not really belonging anywhere or to always feeling alone again in the end. On the physical level a weakness of this energy center shows itself in the feeling of not having enough energy, or feeling weak and sick. At the same time, you might also feel a sense of inner restlessness.

Activating this energy center strengthens your self-confidence in any situation and therefore transforms feelings of insecurity and fear. At the same time, you will feel grounded and stable again, which helps being present in your own physical body. It's all about being able to ground yourself, to focus and to be centered.

Many modern interpretations state that this energy center also has a strong impact on our career and on our financial success. When your base chakra (root chakra) has a lot of energy, then you are in a state where you love what you do and where you are rewarded for your good services. Others may envy you for your ability to earn a lot of money and to save and to invest your money. When you are at a high energy level you will always have more than enough money in order to go on a holiday and to buy the things you like without feeling guilty afterwards. You feel accepted by your friends and you are physically and emotionally at ease with yourself.

However, when this energy center is weakened or blocked, it is believed that this is the reason why we often get stuck in an activity that does not really satisfy us. Somehow we will never have enough money and constantly worry about it. In this state we doubt that we can effectively deal with money. A blockage in this chakra might also lead to weight problems which will further enhance feelings of insecurity.

Exercise 9

Ask yourself: What are your biggest fears?

- -

In which areas of your life are you simply trying to survive?

- -

Focus on your first energy center, on the area of the perineum, whilst chanting. Let these fears completely go whilst you are chanting, knowing that you are fully equipped.

The second energy center (Ge): enjoyment and creativity

This energy center lies on the middle line below the navel and is also called the "sacral chakra". Its color is orange and traditionally it stands for enjoyment,  pleasure, creativity, sexuality and the joy of life.

If this energy center is blocked, then the lymph vessels and blood circulation are "jammed". In this case you feel rather inflexible and unmotivated. Life appears to be boring. Your mood as well as your muscles feel cramped and rigid. On the physical level, there is tension and congestion throughout your whole body, most especially, however, in the lower back. A blockage in this center is often accompanied with bladder and kidney problems. Activating this chakra leads to the feeling of joy rising up, which enables you to enjoy your life more and to be more creative. Physical blockages are resolved and things get moving again.

Modern interpretations emphasize that an activation of this energy center leads to a sharp increase in one's own creativity and helps you to get rid of guilty feelings that prevent you from enjoying life.

Exercise 10

Ask yourself: For what things am I blaming myself?

In which areas of my life do I feel guilty?

- -

When do I feel unworthy?

- -

‹ Focus on your second energy center, on the middle line below your
› navel, whilst chanting. Release those feelings whilst you are
› chanting, knowing that you can transform any situation.

: The third energy center (Ren): power and self-confidence

The third energy center, the so-called "navel · chakra", lies 3-4 centi- ⁕ meters above the navel in ‹ the range of the solar  ⁕ plexus. Its color is yellow and in many traditions it represents the ⁕ strength of our will power, and also of our creativity.

, When the third energy center is blocked, we tend to feel passive › and indecisive. You feel like a frustrated victim of your circum- ⁕ stances. Many old emotions like anger are jammed at this point. ‹ Activating this energy center reinforces your inner strength and ⁴ your own power to assume full responsibility for your own life. Therefore, this energy center may also have a big impact on how successful you are.

Modern interpretations assume that we have strong self- › confidence and high self-esteem if this center of your own personal power has lots of energy. However, if this center is weak • or blocked then we suffer from low self-esteem and feelings of • worthlessness. In this situation you tend to question yourself constantly when it comes to important decisions such as choosing a partner, having children, career changes or moving to another city. You find it difficult to make a decision. In this case you feel more like a victim in this world, often helpless and subject to circumstances. A weakness of this energy center relates to the central nervous system and often shows itself in stomach problems or a feeling of anxiety in the stomach area. Digestive problems, nerve pain and liver disorders might also be the result.

This, along with the first two energy centers, stands for our concrete situation in the material world. According to many traditions it is therefore particularly important to activate and to clean these energy centers in order to be effective in daily life.

Exercise 11

Ask yourself: What am I angry or ashamed of?

- -

When do I feel insecure?

- -

Focus on your third energy center, 3-4 centimeters above the navel, whilst chanting. Let go of these feelings whilst you are chanting, knowing that you can always start new causes in your life.

¦ *The fourth energy center (Hō): love and connectedness*

The fourth energy center,
the so-called "heart
chakra", lies in the center of
the chest at the level of the
heart. Its color is green and
it represents the center of
love and connection with other people.

If this energy center is blocked, then you will feel cut off from others and lonely. We are also separated from our positive emotions. Activating the fourth energy center makes us feel that deep down we are connected to all other people. You no longer feel isolated from others, but a part of the whole, and able to accept yourself totally. You start to have loving and fulfilling feelings. You feel it´s easier to have closer and deeper ties and friendships to others and to deepen existing relationships. The fourth energy center must first be purified in order to be able to listen to the voice of your own higher self.

According to modern interpretations, a weakness or blockage in the fourth energy center causes us to be afraid to lose our autonomy in our relationships, if we trust others too much. In this state we tend to sabotage our relationships with others with mistrust and anger. This creates the fear of binding yourself to others and you often experience quarrels or misunderstandings with the people you love. As a result you constantly try to protect yourself to avoid being hurt.

On the physical level, a weakening of this chakra leads to heart and circulatory problems, poor blood circulation and numbness. Such an energetic blockage is also said to play a role in joint stiffness and the development of breast cancer.

Exercise 12

Ask yourself: What makes me sad?

What losses are bothering me?

Focus on your fourth energy center, on the area of your heart, whilst chanting. Release all feelings of sadness and loss whilst you are chanting, knowing that you are always connected to everything and everybody.

The fifth energy center (Myō): authentic self-expression

The fifth energy center, the so-called "throat chakra", lies in the middle of the neck in the area of the throat. Its color is light blue and represents your own authentic self-expression in any area, such as when you speak, move, write, dance or sing.

If this energy center is blocked, then you have difficulties expressing yourself and inhibitions to express your own opinion in all areas of life. Activating the fifth energy center means that it becomes easier to express yourself clearly and authentically in any form and to tell your own truth. You then reach more harmony through conversations and your own self-expression feels natural.

On a physical level, a blockage of this chakra may also lead to a sore throat, to tension in the shoulders and the neck, to dental problems and to disorders of the thyroid gland.

Exercise 13

Ask yourself: In which situations am I denying myself?

- -

In which areas of my life am I not being honest to myself?

- -

In what ways am I not accepting myself?

- -

Focus on your fifth energy center whilst chanting, in the area of your throat, and release those feelings whilst you are chanting, knowing that you are connected to your true self.

⁞ *The sixth energy center (Mu): intuition and spirituality*

The sixth energy center lies between the eyebrows or slightly above.

Its color is dark blue and symbolizes intuition, spiritual insight and expansion of consciousness.

- If this energy center is blocked, then you may often fall into rigid thought patterns and limiting beliefs. It is then difficult for you to concentrate on one thing and your consciousness is very limited.
- This center can also be blocked by the strong feeling of being separated from everything and everybody. Then you may judge and envy other people. Activating the sixth energy center leads to your consciousness being expanded on a deeper spiritual level. At

this level you begin to intuitively perceive things in a clearer and deeper way.

Modern interpretations suggest that by strengthening this energy center you sense things without exactly knowing how. Intuitively you make the right decisions concerning your family or your career, for example. A strong energy in this center leads to an extreme clarity in everything you do. If this sixth energy center is blocked, then it is difficult for you to make decisions or to evaluate situations or choices. You feel indecisive and you find it difficult to stick to your choices, since you have taken so many wrong deci- sions beforehand. You may miss the access to the spiritual level and you may not exactly know what the real meaning of your life is. On a physical level, a blockage of this energy center may also lead to eye problems, insomnia, or cause headaches and tension in the forehead area.

Exercise 14

Ask yourself: Where do I feel separated?

- -

When do I envy other people?

- -

Focus on your fifth energy center, in the area between your eyebrows, whilst chanting. Release the feeling of being separated whilst you are chanting, knowing that we are all connected to each other.

The seventh energy center (Na): connection to the higher self

The seventh energy center lies at the top of the head and is traditionally called the "crown chakra." Its color is violet and it stands for  the connection to higher levels of consciousness and to one´s higher self.

If the seventh energy center is blocked, then there is a sense of meaninglessness and emptiness. In this case you have lost touch with your higher self and your spiritual source and you only focus on material things. Activating this energy center means that you will begin to feel a cosmic connection and opening, allowing inner peace and harmony and complete acceptance of yourself.

According to modern interpretations a stronger energy in this center shows itself in the feeling of being connected to a higher power or simply to your higher self. In daily life, you are then surrounded by the feeling of being carried safely. The things you need just come to you. This leads to a deep sense of gratitude and a great appreciation of yourself and others.

A blocking and weakening of this energy center means that you may not feel any connection to a higher power and therefore may have the feeling of loneliness. This may manifest in a feeling of deep anger, as if a higher power has abandoned you. Psychological problems may occur, as well as neurological disorders. On a physical level, such a blockage frequently leads to migraine attacks and strong headaches.

Exercise 15

Ask yourself: Where am I too much attached to my outer world? Where do I feel alone?

- -

- -

Focus on your seventh energy center, at the top of your head, whilst chanting and release those feelings, knowing that you are connected to your higher self that never leaves you alone.

The chakras and their associated organs and symptoms

	Chakra	Associated organs/areas	Symptoms of an unbalanced chakra state
1	**Root Chakra**	Reproductive organs, adrenal glands, spine, blood	Weight problems, anxiety, constipation, cramps, fatigue
2	**Sacral Chakra**	Kidney, ovaries, testes, uterus	Pain in the lower back, bladder and kidney problems
3	**Navel Chakra (Solar Plexus)**	Central nervous system, stomach and intestines, liver, pancreas, metabolism	Digestive problems, stomach ulcers, liver problems, nausea, nerve pain
4	**Heart Chakra**	Thymus gland, immune system, heart, lungs, chest	Heart and circulatory problems, heart attack, asthma, breast cancer, stiff joints

5	Throat Chakra	Thyroid, neck, throat, shoulders, ears, mouth	Tensions in the neck and shoulders, sore throat, ear ache, dental and thyroid problems
6	Third Eye Chakra (Intuition)	Pituitary gland, eyes, biorhythms	Eye problems, headaches, migraines, insomnia, nightmares
7	Crown Chakra	Pituitary and pineal glands, cerebral cortex, central nervous system	Dizziness, migraine, confusion, neurological disorders, nerve pain, psychological disorders

Chapter 10
Energy field in surroundings

You are inseparable from your surroundings

We asked ourselves further questions after the measurement of our energy fields and our energy centers. If it is already possible to measure the energetic state of a person and the change of this state, then what is the case with the energetic state of the room this person is in?

Nichiren speaks of the two principles of "inseparability of body and mind" (*shikishin-funi*) and of the "inseparability of the person and his or her environment" (*eshō-funi*).

The principle of the inseparability of the body and mind means the body and your mind form one unit.

In this sense, changing the state of your mind also means to change your energy or your physical state and vice versa. The same is true for your environment.

The principle of the inseparability of the person and their environment says that your mind and the state of your environment depend on each other.

Once the state of your consciousness and thus your energy changes, then the energy of your environment changes. This principle can be experienced by practicing **daimoku.** The effect of **daimoku** shows itself concretely in your own environment. Once I showed an Iranian friend of mine the room in our house in Japan in which we exclusively practiced **daimoku.** She immediately noticed with astonishment that the energy in the room was different than in the other rooms. Since then I realized very consciously that stagnant energy in a room dissolved when you chant intensively in that room.

But was it possible to prove this effect energetically and to depict it as an image? Was it possible to measure the influence of the energy, on your body and also on your environment? We asked ourselves those questions.

We had often noticed that the energy in our daimoku-dōjō, our daimoku practice room, had changed greatly after an intensive hour of chanting. In time this room showed a very special atmosphere characterized by clarity and ease, which was intuitively perceived by our participants.

When I come home at night and open the front door, I immediately know by the atmosphere in the house whether my husband has recently been chanting daimoku intensively. I feel that often, even when I am not at home. I could not explain it, though. Very often I intensely experienced the principle of "inseparability of the person and his or her environment" (eshō-funi) on a personal level. In the course of time, drastic changes can arise in your own personal environment when you are chanting daimoku regularly. Even after a short time, however, one will notice quite a different atmosphere in the room.

We did some research and found out that with GDV measurement it is also possible to measure the energy changes in a room with a special instrument. Thereby the changes in the electromagnetic field of a room are detected. Of course we wanted to try this measurement by any means.

Measuring the energetic change in the room

We had the corresponding measurement devices installed before our ten-minute daimoku. These devices then recorded the changes in the electromagnetic field of the room that occurred during our daimoku recitation. Afterwards, these devices remained on for another ten minutes, in order to find out whether the room had changed again energetically after the **daimoku** recitation.

The result impressed us. In the ten minutes during which we had been chanting **daimoku** together, the energetic structure of the room had changed dramatically. This showed a sharp increase of the electromagnetic oscillations in the room. This is shown in the following picture by the red (above) lines. Sometime after finishing **daimoku**, the energy of the room fell again to a lower level, as is indicated by the blue lines. The blue (below) lines probably show the original energy output level of the room. **Daimoku** had the power to significantly increase the energy in the room and to change the electromagnetic fields in the room.

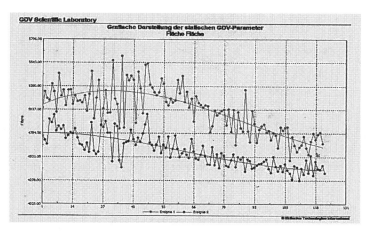

Room measurement during and after daimoku

The following graph of the measurement shows the great increase of energy in the room and the change of the structure of the room that occurred during the

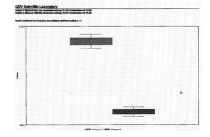

recitation. The daimoku had greatly increased the energetic indoor climate of the room.

> With daimoku you can immediately raise
> the energy in the room strongly.

Increase and clean the energy of your environment

Is the atmosphere of the place where you chant to the Gohonzon conducive to your inner creation process? Do you feel safe there and does this place lift your mood? These feelings affect the vibration you send out whilst you are chanting. The place where you are chanting to the Gohonzon should feel like a "sacred place" that supports your creative process.

The vibration of the daimoku can clean a room effectively and powerfully. It transforms stagnant, heavy or negative energy in a room. Just mentally direct some daimoku into the larger, more open areas of the room and then specifically into the area that feels heavy. You can also chant internally when you are in a situation where thick air or a bad mood prevails. Even in the office you can chant daimoku internally when you have a problem with your boss or your colleagues. This applies to any other difficult situation.

The unfolding of Buddhahood is an energetic process

The most important aspect of the energetic approach to the practice of daimoku is that we are talking about an energetic process that is carried out again and again. The unfolding of Buddhahood is also an energetic process that shows its effect both momentarily as well as permanently. Thus you are able to align yourself to the energy of the superior energy field, independent of your own current situation. A change of our own energy leads to changes in our environment.

During the deep fusion with the Mandala-Gohonzon we synchronize our own energy field with the superior, higher-frequency field of energy and consciousness. Through this we experience the phenomenon of "downloading" energy from this field. This was demonstrated even after ten minutes of **daimoku.** The higher vibrating energy of the superior energy field had dissolved the energy blockages of compressed energy and thus "refilled" my energy field. The measurements of the energy of the room had also shown that this process of energy increase represents a temporarily process. After **daimoku** recitation the energy of the room falls back to a lower level. In the same way your own energy field falls back to the level that corresponds to your karmic tendency. That is why it is so important to regularly increase your own energy field and to synchronize it with the superior energy field on a daily basis.

Exercise 16

Think of the Ninth Consciousness as a higher field that is complete and full of energy!

This field is not interested in your past behavior.

Your past is completely irrelevant when it comes to connecting to this field.

Chapter 11
Energized Water Crystal Pictures

The energy of daimoku made visible

In his book "The Hidden Messages of Water", Japanese researcher Masaru Emoto argues that water is a kind of energy carrier that receives the vibrations of words, characters and even thoughts and feelings, and reflects them in a visible form. Through his photographs he showed how people´s emotions changed the water according to their different state of life and how the water reflects and also stores the energy of those people. Using high-speed photography Emoto shows that the crystals of frozen water take completely different forms depending on what feelings or energies are directed to the water. Emoto found that water that has been exposed to loving words shows brilliant, complex, and colorful snowflake patterns. In contrast, water that is exposed to negative thoughts forms incomplete, asymmetrical patterns with dull colors. Thus, an ugly pattern forms after feelings of hatred, anger and negativity were directed towards the water. On the contrary, a wonderful crystalline structure is formed when feelings of gratitude and love are projected onto the water. If you imagine that the human body is 70-80% water, then you should ask yourself: which one of the two patterns do you prefer in your body?

"You make me sick, I will kill you!"

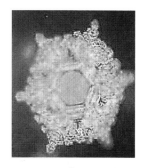

Love and Gratitude

These images "make it clear to our eyes" that negative emotions and states of life that are influenced by the emotions of anger and hatred really are "mind poison" in the truest sense of the word. For this reason you should be very aware of what you "send out" as inner images, ideas, thoughts and words.

In the case of the water crystal photographs, water is exposed to a certain vibration in the form of music, words or prayers and then frozen, in order to be photographed. These images also show that H_2O converts vibrations into a visible form and therefore it may also be possible to create images of cosmic forces that are generated by the sound of a mantra to which the water is exposed to.

Energizing water with Nam-myō-hō-ren-ge-kyō

We did some research on this phenomenon and tested the effect of **daimoku** (i.e. of the mantra Nam-myō-hō-ren-ge-kyō) on water, in order to make the energy structure of this mantra visible. The basis was distilled water, because studies have shown that distilled water itself does not form any symmetrical water crystals and has the lowest number of impurities.

Distilled water does not form any symmetrical water crystals unless energized with positive energy.

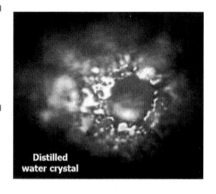

Distilled water crystal

We therefore used a bottle of distilled water and energized it with **daimoku**. We put it in front of the mandala inscribed by Nichiren so that the water could absorb the energy signature of this mandala. Then we recited the mantra "Nam-myō-hō-ren-ge-kyō" in a deeply focused manner. Afterwards we had an institute follow the method developed by Dr. Masaru Emoto produce water crystal photography of the water.

The result was a beautiful hexagonal water crystal that clearly shows that the energy and vibration of daimoku and the energy of the Gohonzon had transformed the distilled water into a magnificent crystal. This was a way to make the mental, emotional and spiritual dimension of daimokupower, or the highest enlightened life state, visible in the outer world.

This makes it clear that the mantra "Nam-myō-hō-ren-ge-kyō" has the power to act on matter, on our body and on our environment and that it has the power to change your energetic state and to influence outer reality. It illustrates the difference if the water in your body or the energy of your surroundings reflect your destructive and disharmonious states, or whether they "shine" in a state transformed by DaimokuPower.

The DaimokuPower Star

We called the water crystal that was developed using energization with daimoku and with Nichiren's Gohonzon the "DaimokuPower Star" because it shines like a bright light in the darkness and makes the clarity, brightness and beauty of this mantra visible. The DaimokuPower Star is a light in the dark and shows clearly that daimoku works.

This image makes it easier to keep the power of daimoku in mind in heavy and in troubled times. The DaimokuPower Star counteracts any doubt and any hopelessness we may have, because it shows us the luminous state we create by activating the enlightened state of life. This way you can motivate yourself any time that you are filled with doubt about whether you can really change your situation: Yes, you can. The DaimokuPower Star gives you a visible proof:

Nam Myo Ho Ren Ge Kyo
©2012 Dr. Susanne Matsudo-Kiliani

DaimokuPower works!

Bibliography

Broers, Dieter: *Gedanken erschaffen Realität - Die Gesetze des Bewusstseins*, München, 2013.

Chamberland, Nyudo: *Quantum Life – Man as Creator Eternal*, Tupelo Mississipi, USA, 2005.

Davies, Brenda: *Chakras - Tore zur Seele*, München, 2007.

Deepak, Chopra: *Das Tor zu vollkommenem Glück*, Knaur Verlag, München, 2004.

Dispenza, Joe: Breaking the habit of being yourself – How to lose your mind and create a new one, Hayhouse UK Ltd, 2012.

Dürr, Hans-Peter: *Geist, Kosmos und Physik*. Crotona Verlag, Amerang, 2010.

Ders.: *Es gibt keine Materie*, Crotona Verlag, Amerang, 2012

Emoto, Masaru: *Wasserkristalle*, Tokio, 2001.

Ders.: *Wasser und die Kraft des Gebets*, Burgrain, 2010

Farwell, Larry: *How Consciousness Commands Matter*, Fairfield, Iowa, 1999.

Ikeda, Daisaku: *Das Prinzip Hoffnung, Goshovorlesungen*, Fata Morgana Verlag, Berlin 2010.

Janzer, Alexander: *Chakras für Anfänger*, Wroclaw, 2013.

Korotkov, Konstantin: *Human Energy Field, Study with GDV Bio-electrography*, Fair Lawn, NJ USA, 2002.

Ders.: *Geheimnisse des lebendigen Leuchtens*, Leipzig 2005.

Lipton, Bruce: *Intelligente Zellen – Wie Erfahrungen unsere Gene steuern*. Burgrain, 10. Aufl., 2006.

McTaggart, Lynn: *Das Nullpunktfeld – Auf der Suche nach der kosmischen Ur-Energie*, München, 2007.

Ders.: *The Bond – Wie in unserer Quantenwelt alles mit allem verbunden ist*, München 2011.

Matsudo, Yukio und Matsudo-Kiliani, Susanne: *Durchbruch mit Daimoku-Power – Einführung in den Nichiren-Buddhismus*, Norderstedt, 2012.

Matsudo, Yukio: *Nichiren, der Ausübende des Lotos-Sutra*, Norderstedt 2004 (Taschenbuch 2009)

Moorjani, Anita: *Heilung im Licht – Wie ich durch eine Nahtoderfahrung den Krebs besiegte und neu geboren wurde*, München, 5. Aufl., 2012.

Pierrakos, John: *Core Energetik – Zentrum Deiner Lebenskraft*, Essen, 1987.

Rothenbücher, Claus: *Die Natur von Realität – das Leben als interaktiver Prozess des Erschaffens*, Bielefeld, 2013.

Stelzl, Diethard: *Geist ist stärker als Materie – Quantenphysik und paranormale Phänomene*, Darmstadt 2014.

Warnke, Ulrich: *Quantenphilosophie und Spiritualität – Der Schlüssel zu den Geheimnissen des menschlichen Seins*, München, 2011.

Ders.: *Quantenphilosophie und Interwelt, Der Zugang zur verborgenen Essenz des menschlichen Wesens*, München, 2013.

About the Authors

Susanne Matsudo-Kiliani, Dr. Phil.

University degree as translator for English and Spanish, PhD in Translation Studies and Religious Studies specializing in Buddhism, Heidelberg University. Certified trainer for Intercultural Competence in International Business.

Dr. Matsudo-Kiliani has been practicing Nichiren Buddhism since 1998 and has experienced many beneficial transformations in her life, which still continue. As a passionate practitioner she has been engaged in building a bridge between Buddhist practice and modern sciences that are now integrating energy and consciousness.

Being a member of the council of the German Buddhist Union (DBU e. V.), she also acts as representative for interreligious dialogue at a federal level for a better mutual understanding among different religions.

Yukio Matsudo, Dr. Phil. Habil.

PhD in Philosophy and post-doc qualification for professorship (Habilitation) in the subjects of Japanese Buddhism and Comparative Religions, Heidelberg University.

After receiving his post-doc qualification, he was active as a lecturer at

Heidelberg University on the subjects of Japanese Buddhism and Comparative Religions from 2001-2014.

Dr. Matsudo has been practicing Nichiren Buddhism intensively since 1976 and was a top leader of SGI Germany at a federal level until 2001. He has supported hundreds of people in their practice. This way he could also gain many concrete and important experiences.

SGI-President Ikeda asked him personally to found and run as Director of Research the European Centre of the Institute of Oriental Philosophy (IOP) in Taplow Court, UK. In this period from 1990-2000, based on the modern, humanistic and open-minded approach of Daisaku Ikeda, he developed an innovative understanding of Nichiren Buddhist teachings and published a number of books and articles in Japanese, German and English.

Today, Dr. Matsudo is engaged in building a bridge between Buddhism, Western philosophy and new scientific disciplines. As an expert in Nichiren Buddhist Studies He is also active in a research group in Japan, in which prominent scholars are represented from all main denominations of Nichiren schools including Soka Gakkai (IOP).

About Our Projects and Publications

We are developing a systematic understanding of Nichiren Buddhism for spiritual transformation as well as for fulfillment of your sincere desires in every aspect of life. Thus, our research results and publications will be only inspiring and deepening your practice of chanting daimoku. In this regard our project comprises three major areas in which we explain the application of Nichiren Buddhism.

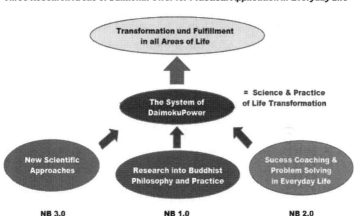

Three Research Areas of DaimokuPower for Practical Application in Everyday Life

1: *Research into Buddhist Philosophy* – In this area we are examining Nichiren Buddhism in terms of its historical and philosophical development and in the meantime we have developed a systematic interpretation which is most suitable to a modern understanding of the practice of self-realization based on the ethic of self-responsibility.

2. *Practical Application* - The area of practically applying Nichiren Buddhism for realizing your visions and improving your life

situation in order to achieve a successful and happy life. In this area we offer effective techniques and methods from areas such as positive psychology, neuro-linguistic programming, success principles, and other areas of consciousness and brain research.

3. *Building a Bridge Between Science and Spirituality* - This area covers new scientific approaches that are now beginning to integrate energy and consciousness, such as quantum physics, electrophotonics, bio-feedback, and epigenetics, as well as research on brain, heart, cell, consciousness including its relation to meditation practice. Fascinatingly, all these new approaches support many concepts and principles developed in Nichiren Buddhism.

All the various aspects of these three pillars are synergetically used for a systematic understanding and exercise of **DaimokuPower** in order for you to achieve transformation and fulfillment in all areas of your life.

Classification for the Series of Publications

Our newly developed, innovative concept and orientation for Nichiren Buddhist study and practice will be delivered according to the above-mentioned research areas. Each of the publications will therefore be classified by its series number and version number like, for example, "Nichiren Buddhism 1.0" (NB 1.0). These classifications do not mean that later versions are revised or better, but that they just belong to different areas or subjects relating to the teachings and practice of Nichiren Buddhism.

1. **The first series** is directly related to the buddhological discussion on Nichiren Buddhism and is called "Nichiren Buddhism 1.0" (NB 1.0). In this series three books have already been published in German*:

- *Nichiren, der Ausübende des Lotos-Sūtra* [Nichiren, the Votary of the Lotus Sutra]. Norderstedt 2004 (Paperback 2009).

- *Hairetischer Protest – Eine vergleichende Studie über buddhistische und christliche reformatorische Bewegungen* [Hairetic Protest – A comparative Study on Buddhist and Christian Reformist Movements]. Norderstedt 2009.

- *Durchbruch mit DaimokuPower – Einführung in den Nichiren-Buddhismus* [Breakthrough with DaimokuPower – An introduction to Nichiren Buddhism]. Norderstedt 2012.

* Several books and articles by Yukio Matsudo have also been published in Japanese. It is still under consideration whether and how we are going to publish a collection of this series in English. For the time being, the above-mentioned topics are also covered by the book **NB 2.1**, which will soon be published in English.

2. **The second series** of publications will be prepared as follows:

NB 2.0   *Activate your unlimited source of happiness.*
         Nichiren Buddhism 2.0

NB 2.1   *Everything you need to know about DaimokuPower.*
         Nichiren Buddhism 2.1

NB 2.2   *Seven steps to successfully practicing DaimokuPower.*
         Nichiren Buddhism 2.2

3. **The third series** refers to modern scientific topics and approaches that show how consciousness and energy are deeply related and which substantiate Buddhist concepts. For demonstrating the meditative and the energetic effects of daimoku on your body, brain and environment the results of some significant measurements will be presented and explained.

NB 3.0   *Transform Your Energy – Change Your Life.*
         Nichiren Buddhism 3.0

NB 3.1   *Design Your Life with DaimokuPower.*
         Nichiren Buddhism 3.1

Contemplation of the Eightfold Path

(Optional, may be used for a period of guided silent meditation prior to Odaimoku chanting or used during Odaimoku chanting to focus one's intention. Contemplate each line while chanting for one full breath cycle.)

May I View the World of the One Reality, the Great Vehicle.

May my Intentions be generous and compassionate.

May my Speech or silences be skillful.

May my Actions be beneficial.

May my Livelihood be wholesome.

May my Efforts move towards wholesome activities and mind-states.

May I be always Mindful.

May I make time every day for Concentration practice.

Ichinen Sanzen in a Nutshell

The Ten Worlds

Hell, Hungry Spirits, Animals, Anger, Humanity, Heaven, Śrāvakas, Pratyekabuddhas, Bodhisattvas, and Buddhahood

multiplied by

The Ten Worlds

Hell, Hungry Spirits, Animals, Anger, Humanity, Heaven, Śrāvakas, Pratyekabuddhas, Bodhisattvas, and Buddhahood

multiplied by

The Ten Aspects

Appearance, Nature, Entity, Power, Activity, Primary Cause, Environmental Cause, Effect, Reward and Retribution, and Equality Despite Theses Differences

multiplied by

The Three Factors

Land, Other Beings, and Components of Self

Instant Enlightenment is the Fusion of Wisdom and Actuality in all 10 dimensions

10. Buddha Compassionate Love for All
Shakyamuni Wisdom : Tenno Actuality

Tamon-ten N **5. Human Calm Rational**	**Nan** **Mu** **Myo** **6. Heavenly Rapture, Joy**	**Jikoku-ten** E **7. Voice Hearers Learning**
Aizen Myoo Rage Ten Worlds **4. Asura Manipul. Arrogance**	**Ho** **Ren** **Ge** **9. Bodhisattva Compassion**	**Fudo Myoo** Unshakable **8. Cause Realization**
Zocho-ten S **3. Animal Instincts**	**Kyo** **Nichi** **Ren** **2. Hungry Spirit Craving Desire**	**Komoku-ten** W **1. Suffering Hell**

Treasure Tower

Personal Prayer

(Optional, may be offered during
Dedication of Merit where noted)

●

I understand my words have meaning and will affect good or harm in others. I vow to turn away from selfish impulses, let go of negativity and cultivate selfless ways of being so that I can be generous with my things, my time and my energy, trustworthy and self-disciplined so that I do not harm others or myself, and patient and compassionate with other beings.

I vow to transform poisons into medicines so that:
Greed becomes Generosity
Fear becomes Courage
Anxiety becomes Tranquility
Anger becomes Patience
Rage becomes Forgiveness
Hate becomes Loving Kindness
Ignorance becomes Wisdom
Arrogance becomes Humility
Doubt and Distraction become Concentration and Mindfulness.

I understand that each and every moment is another opportunity for me to practice the Eightfold Path and the Six Perfections.

Made in the USA
San Bernardino, CA
19 January 2020